"In *Leading Morale*, Kate Nasser not only informs us about the importance of morale in a successful workplace, but also gives us tactical steps to effectively define and lead morale in diverse organizations. Kate reminds us of what is too often forgotten—leading morale is not an event or simply being nice to people, but positive actions and words, working in unison, to empower and engage employees at all levels. *Leading Morale* is filled with checklists, discussion starters, and self-assessments that will help leaders transform their teams and organizations."

—Alli Polin, Consultant, Coach,
Co-Author, *Energize Your Leadership*

"Morale is a traditional concept that is still relevant but in need of a refresh. *Leading Morale* revives the importance of morale with contemporary practices and actionable steps for current and the next generation of leaders."

—Jon Mertz, Founder of Thin Difference,
a cross-generational leadership community

"*Leading Morale* is a powerful guided exercise into leadership awareness. Kate Nasser goes beyond the typical morale literature, asking the tough questions to make people realize everyone has a role to play when it comes to creating and sustaining an empowered workplace.

From the moment I began reading *Leading Morale*, I felt as though I had Kate alongside with me, providing me with a one-on-one consultation. The book is a powerful exercise in self-awareness and how each person truly affects workplace culture."

—Andrea Sanchez, Founder and Chief,
SparkStory, LLC

Leading Morale

The People Skills
to Stop Negativity
& Ignite Contributions

Kate Nasser
The People Skills Coach™

Published by:
CAS, Inc.
Somerville, NJ 08876
https:/KateNasser.com

ISBN: 978-1-7321007-0-1
Library of Congress Control Number: 2018903484

Printed in the United States of America.

Cover design by Kimb Williams Graphic Design, Canada.

This book is dedicated to all the workplace leaders, managers, and teams who commit to conquering great challenges to achieve the heights of success.

I give special thanks to all my conference participants and clients over these 25+ years who trusted me to help them overcome their leadership and teamwork obstacles. Your unique challenges have inspired me to even greater depths of curiosity and learning. Your willingness to use my insights to change how you work together has sustained my desire to write this book. I am honored and grateful to have worked with each of you.

Lastly, I thank my mom who during my formative years focused constantly on how you treat others. This seeped into every part of my being and ultimately shaped my final career choice as The People Skills Coach.™

I now offer you this book of insights on Leading Morale.

Contents

Introduction
xvii

CHAPTER ONE
Define Morale to Lead Morale
1

CHAPTER TWO
Get Comfortable Giving Praise
9

CHAPTER THREE
Be Courageously Self-Aware
15

CHAPTER FOUR
Are You Comfortable With Emotion?
31

CHAPTER FIVE
Use the Power of Courtesy and Communication
43

CHAPTER SIX
Address Chronic Complaining and Negativity
53

CHAPTER SEVEN
Breed Accountability, Not Blame
61

CHAPTER EIGHT
Highlight Individual Talents
67

CHAPTER NINE
Influence, Don't Manipulate
75

CHAPTER TEN
Address Bad Behaviors
85

CHAPTER ELEVEN
Treat Employees the Way They Want to Be Treated
103

CHAPTER TWELVE
Now It's Up to You
111

Conclusion—From Beginning to End
135

References
139

Acknowledgments
141

About the Author
143

Your Indulgence Please

I have taken the liberty of using the plural pronouns "they, their, them" in cases where traditional grammar rules require a singular pronoun such as s/he, his/her. I have done this because using the singular would break the conversational tone of the book. Moreover, "their" is an inclusive term and inclusiveness is key to morale!

I ask your indulgence of this liberty I have taken and thank you for your understanding.

As you read this book, think of ONE word:

DIGNITY

Underneath it all, morale is all about dignity.

*If you aren't leading morale,
you aren't leading anyone!*

Introduction

Do you lead morale? No? Why not? Is it because you didn't think about it until now? Or you believe that morale is not something anyone can lead? Or you think that as a leader you should delegate that to someone else? Or you are concerned that it will distract and detract from reaching results? Or you believe it won't work for you and those you lead? Or you don't care about morale? Or you don't think employees care about it? Well they do and consider this:

If you aren't leading morale, you aren't leading anyone.

There are leaders who see leading morale as the softer side (i.e. less important) part of leadership. It isn't. It is a critical component of leadership and success. That is why this book explores leading morale. It is not a book with 101 games, events, and celebrations to pump people up. Those books have been written and have value. Yet despite their value, they have also contributed to the view that morale is about moments and events. It isn't.

Consider this first-hand account from Christy K. on how her leaders made this big mistake:

> *I worked for a large agency and the leaders demeaned people. The office had plenty of free snacks, special events like bring your dog to work day, and even kegs of beer. The leaders even took us on exotic trips. Yet they always demeaned us and attacked us. On the trips, they shot nerf guns at us and then they were insulted and upset when we didn't want to eat dinner with them. It was no surprise that turnover was high. Morale is not about free food, free beer, and free trips while being demeaned every day.*

I couldn't agree with you more Christy. Moreover, morale isn't occasional moments in time. It needs to be there all the time. Morale is not the same as daily mood. Morale sustains leaders and teams to reach goals despite bad moods. Morale is at the heart of employee engagement. It impacts accountability, agility, innovation, productivity, and profitability. Morale affects successful change and success overall. It isn't a nice-to-have; it's a must have.

> **Morale isn't a nice-to-have; it's a must have!**

Leading morale is all about the deeper fabric of what keeps employees, teams, and organizations inspired, enthused, committed, engaged, and productive to reach results in good times and bad.

In "The People Power of Transformation" (McKinsey Quarterly Feb. 2017), Senior Partner, Dana Maor et al. highlight why engaged employees are critical for transforming company success.

In The Neuroscience of Trust, (Harvard Business Review Jan.-Feb. 2017) Paul Zak highlights that the "Gallup organization analyzed years and years of data showing that high engagement consistently leads to positive outcomes for individuals and organizations including higher productivity, better-quality products, and increased profitability."

In my 25+ years of consulting to companies of all sizes, I can attest that leading morale feeds and sustains the high engagement these studies reference.

Morale doesn't just happen. You must lead it. What does just happen without leaders noticing is bad morale. They often dismiss early signs of bad morale as simple personality conflicts, bad culture fit, temporary reactions to workplace stress, or passing moods. Then suddenly the morale problems and negativity hit them in the face. As a consultant who goes into companies to address morale, I see the signs that leaders have missed or dismissed. Those leaders face the much more difficult task of fixing morale.

You don't have to be one of those blind leaders. This book is all about how to lead morale with the people skills to stop negativity and ignite contributions. It brings you my 25+ years of practical experience with leading morale so you won't have to struggle to fix it later. Of course there are many books on leadership and several books about boosting morale. Yet there is little written on leading morale instead of boosting it. This book fills that void and gives you the roadmap to success.

The road map begins with meeting a universal human need—respect. Everyone wants it. That's why respect is the cornerstone of morale. Respect communicates a sense of worth and tells people they matter as human beings and as employees. Since everybody wants to know they matter, you cannot lead morale without showing respect. Consider why comedian Rodney Dangerfield's signature line, *I get no respect*, hooked so many people. It was that universal plea for respect.

Start leading morale by showing basic human respect through all your words and actions. It lays the foundation of morale. Everyone can earn additional respect for commitment and accomplishments. Yet you must show basic human respect to everyone to lead morale. For those who claim that the only things an employee wants are a job and a paycheck, I urge them to look at how many paid employees in diverse companies have mediocre or low morale. Clearly, it takes more than money to create morale.

Leading morale must also focus on belonging. To belong is to be valued and connected not just present and silent. Belonging, a human social need, represents acceptance in the organization. In an article, "Why Belonging is Key in Today's Workplace", (Digitalist Magazine, Dec. 2014), consultant Lisa Shelley notes research from Lieberman, Eisenhower, 2008 that "the brain uses similar circuits to handle the social and physical variants of pain and pleasure." In other words, the brain addresses the social need for survival (belonging) in a similar manner as it does physical need for survival. Lisa rightly concludes that "anxiety, avoidance of tasks and uncooperative or even undermining behavior can result when the (workplace) environment indicates threats to social needs."

To lead morale, remember that the employees' social need to belong is just as strong as the physical need to survive. We will cover more on this later in this book.

Leading morale must also create a sense of strength, confidence, and know-how to reach objectives and overcome difficulties. This is why providing training and growth opportunities is essential in sustaining employee morale.

Added to all of this, especially with the new generations in the workplace, is a sense of meaning at work. Many companies have this as a goal today. One of the most valuable resources on this topic is the article "Increasing the Meaning Quotient of Work" in McKinsey Quarterly Jan. 2013. In it Susie Cranston, McKinsey senior expert and Scott Keller, Director in San Francisco, highlight why common approaches to inspiring employees fail. They also note the research indicating what approach will increase the meaning quotient at work.

So as you start your journey through this book, remember that morale is about dignity, respect, trust, belonging, know how, meaning at work, and growth opportunities. Fun events and awards are intermittent expressions of that. Alone, they do not lead morale.

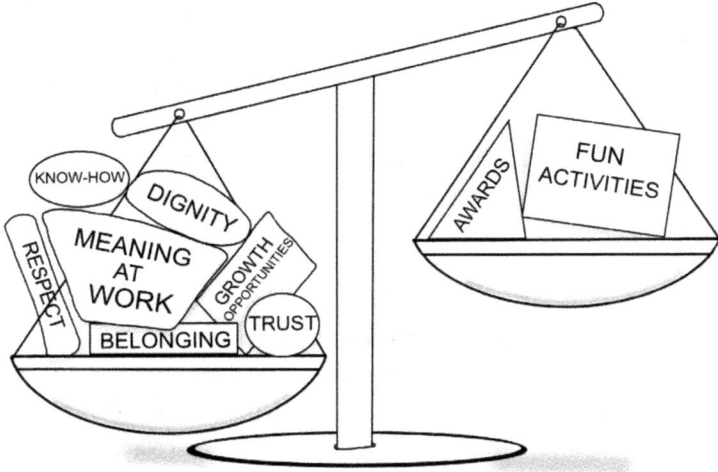

© 2018 Kate Nasser, CAS, Inc.

1

Define morale.
It is not an event
or single moments
in time.

CHAPTER ONE

Define Morale to Lead Morale

What image does the word leader create in your mind: a) Confident, courageous, objective, clear thinking, no nonsense decision maker or b) Confident, courageous, objective, clear thinking, engager who inspires the teams to contribute their full talents and empowers them to develop into leaders?

Historically (a) was the picture of a leader. Leaders directed people's actions to produce results. Everyone was expected to follow the organization's leaders. The focus was not on morale nor was leading morale on the list of what leaders must do. People didn't go to work thinking primarily about their morale. They went to work to earn a living and have security. They often stayed with the same company for that reason.

How do you define leadership?

Fast forward to today. The workplace is very different. Decades of companies downsizing and outsourcing have erased the picture of employees' sacrificing their needs for a lifetime of security at a company. Employees now think about how they feel at work. Younger generations place a high value on quality of life in and outside of work.

The image of leadership must now include leading morale. Morale affects people's engagement—contributions and performance. Morale affects teamwork and collaboration, both essential to results in a non-assembly line workplace. Morale affects retention of the talent and skills you hire. Since leadership now focuses on engaging and empowering, it must also focus on leading morale.

As leaders, you cannot delegate the role of morale to Human Resources or to one person in your own organization. Every move you make, every step you take, every word you utter affects morale. Lead it, model it, monitor it. Otherwise you will be stuck fixing it when you suddenly discover your organization has a morale problem. So what does it take to lead morale?

First define morale.

Do you or your employees define it as:

- Constant happiness? Hopefully not. No one is happy all the time.

- Individual choice without boundaries or responsibilities? Not a very realistic definition. Work has boundaries and obligations.

- Unbounded optimism? This might be a hard sell to the self-professed realists on your teams.

- Unanimous agreement at all times? A mind chilling idea and a dangerous step because it produces group think and blinds people to business risks and challenges.

- Cheerleading event that pumps everyone up? Morale is not an event.

Morale is the state of mind relating to confidence, enthusiasm, purpose, and discipline toward goals. More simply, the spirit of a group that makes the members want to be in the group and make the group succeed.

Defining it is very important. Many leaders resist leading morale because of what they assume it is. If you or your employees assume that the definition is any of the bullet points noted above, this hidden assumption can block your desire to lead morale and also your ability to do it.

Action Step: Create a definition of morale with your employees. Every organization needs a shared, working definition of morale. It lets team members know that you believe morale is important enough to lead and important enough for everyone to maintain. It then opens discussions about everyone's role in morale.

Define morale *with* your employees.

Involve them in creating this shared definition. It helps everyone think through what morale is and what it isn't. This is key to leading and maintaining great morale.

At the beginning, don't get stuck in debates about which words to use. Capture what everyone thinks without spending hours worrying about the perfect way to write it. Let the thinking flow. You can clean up the wording later.

Some questions to guide your discussions on what is morale:

- What picture does the word morale create in your mind?

- How does morale affect us and our work?

- Is morale something we consciously build or does it just happen?

- What mindset or beliefs must we live to sustain good morale?

- Can we disagree on issues and still have good morale? Why/why not?

- What are some examples of behaviors or beliefs that build morale and those that hurt morale?

- Who is responsible for individual morale: the individual, the team, or the leader?

- What is the difference between good morale and constant happiness, if any?

Engaging team members in defining morale unearths positive insights and potentially harmful assumptions. You will all learn a great deal about each other during these discussions. Everyone has the chance to work through different views. Everybody starts to see that the team's morale is everyone's responsibility. As you lead morale, team members begin to own it and become co-leaders of it.

As the discussions progress, be ready to clarify some of the more common misunderstandings about morale:

Difference between morale and constant happiness.

Constant happiness for some people means the absence of: struggle, disappointment, hard work, and compromise. For others it means getting everything they want when they want it. Morale, on the other hand, is the enthusiasm and discipline to work with others to achieve a shared purpose. It's grit in the face of struggle, confidence in the face of challenges. As a leader you can lead the team to develop enthusiasm, discipline, even grit. You cannot guarantee constant happiness.

Who is responsible for individual mood, the leader or the individual?

I submit to you that an individual is responsible for their own mood. We each have a life and we must do things to stay positive and enthusiastic in our individual lives.

Yet as noted in the introduction, mood is not the same as morale. Morale is the collective spirit to overcome bad moods and other challenges in order to reach team success.

Leaders must lead morale. You can't say that it's up to the individual because what you do as a leader impacts morale. Company decisions impact morale. The culture you feed and lead impacts morale. The culture that you allow to develop affects morale. What the team does in that culture impacts morale. Ignoring all of that and claiming it is purely an individual responsibility leads to morale problems and turnover.

How can we disagree and still have good morale?

It's not what you say; it's how you say it. Civility doesn't weaken your message. It helps others hear it. Every person wants basic human respect not disdain. When everyone shows respect even in disagreement, it sustains morale. Model honesty with civility and you lead this effort. More on this later in the chapter on courtesy and civility.

What do we do when someone is lax and we as teammates have to pick up the slack?

This issue, left unaddressed, undercuts morale. Team members who take extra long lunches and breaks, start work late and leave early on a regular basis burden others. These actions also communicate lack of respect to teammates. These teammates may even start to feel they're being played for fools.

If these teammates come to you, the leader, how will you respond? Will you tell them to just handle it themselves? This can undercut morale. If they do handle it themselves and the lax team member says, "Mind your own business, you're not my boss", it undercuts morale.

Discussing this question as part of the definition of morale will uncover team members' views and help prevent morale trouble.

What do we do when a top performer doesn't collaborate or share knowledge?

The top performing maverick is one sign of morale trouble that leaders often dismiss. They see the productivity and close their eyes to how the maverick's behavior impacts morale. More on high performing mavericks later in this book.

What issues does the team want to raise during this morale definition session?

Ask participants what other important issues affect morale. You can differentiate between slight annoyances and deeper issues that impact the enthusiasm, discipline, and spirit to get things done. This step teaches you about what inspires and discourages those you lead. It also continues to show them that they must participate in maintaining morale.

Don't assume everyone defines morale the same way.
As the old saying goes, when you assume you make an
Ass... out of... U... and Me!

2

*Get comfortable
giving praise and celebrating
people's talents.*

CHAPTER TWO

Get Comfortable Giving Praise

No definition or a poor definition of morale is only one reason why leaders don't lead morale.

They also claim:

- "I don't have time." They say they are working on the business not in the business. In truth they have time. They choose to use their time on issues other than morale. They delegate morale to someone else. Yet it is doomed to fail because the message is, morale is not important enough for the leader to lead.

- "Morale is not something you can create. It just happens. You can only fix it when it's broken." This is not true. In fact, there are extreme cases when you cannot fix bad morale. However, you can always build it from scratch and maintain it.

- "Morale is touchy feely and applies only to super sensitive people. Focusing on it sidetracks success and results." Not true. Actually morale applies to everyone. You will be hard pressed to find people who are not affected by morale. Morale is the daily pulse and pathway to success.

- "Focusing on morale makes people weak. Toughen them up and they perform better." Ironically, focusing on morale builds the strength and resolve to face tough challenges.

Leaders who don't lead morale, avoid it because:

- They are uncomfortable with positive emotion and getting close to people. They have lower emotional intelligence. They cringe at the thought of anything related to emotion.

Example: An internal technical support rep in a major corporation had a very good work ethic, great technical skills, and outstanding customer service people skills. She went to assist an employee with a technical problem. She fixed it. The employee was thrilled. As the support rep's VP walked by, the employee whom the rep had helped said to the VP, "She is great. She is always here when we need her and she gets us working again." The VP replied, "Maybe that's why she can't get her own work done."

> **You don't have to be a cheerleader to lead morale.**

Solving employees' technical problems was this support rep's work and she had top-notch performance reviews. The VP's snide remark was out of place and hurt morale. He knew the rep's performance was outstanding. He was uncomfortable hearing glowing comments about his staff and uncomfortable saying something positive in front of her.

Lesson for leaders: You don't have to be a cheerleader to lead morale. You do have to be comfortable with praise and with expressing positive emotion.

- They believe they don't have the personality for it.

Driver type personalities who live for results picture leading morale as a secondary activity. They even tell themselves they don't have the personality for it. If you are a driver personality, remember that if you want results from non-driver types, you must lead morale. It's not secondary. It's essential.

Some introverts believe that they cannot lead morale. They see leading morale as an extroverted energy-draining activity and they cringe at the thought of it. If you are an introverted leader (and yes they do exist), picture all the elements of morale that you can be very good at leading: communicating with respect, sharing credit for results vs. hogging it all, listening to team members' ideas, being flexible to change, sharing your insights when team members get stuck. Leading morale is no more demanding than the other aspects of leadership. Continue to work on the challenges of leadership communication; don't convince yourself you cannot lead morale. Lisa Petrilli's book, *An Introvert's Guide to Success in Business and Leadership,* can guide you with additional insights.

- They fear they will be trapped in employees' emotions or that they can never achieve great morale.

When you picture leading morale, what picture do you see? What thoughts jump to your mind? Is your first reaction that you don't want to babysit employees? Do you picture being trapped in people's emotions or in endless complaints?

"I've fallen into being nice and I can't get up!"

© 2018 Kate Nasser, CAS, Inc.

Ask yourself, why is this your image? Why such a fearful negative picture? Is it because you haven't seen positive morale in action? Or are you uncomfortable with positive emotion even in your personal life?

Leading morale is all about inspiring positive attitudes, enthusiasm, commitment, and discipline to achieve results—and that takes positive emotion. If you don't lead morale, you will be trapped in trying to fix it later. Lead it so you won't have to fix it. If morale is currently broken, reach out to consultants, like me, to help restart your teams on a new path. An outsider's perspective breathes new life into morale.

- They are concerned that leading morale will make them look weak.

  Draw a picture of a leader you would want to work for. Now draw a picture of yourself as leader. If you are not a visual thinker, list out the leadership behaviors you admire instead of drawing the picture. Then list out your leadership strengths and those you need to work on. Now review the pictures or your lists. Do they include elements of great communication, positive feedback, and engaging employees? Or is the overall image skewed toward toughness and results? The first image leads morale; the second one avoids it. The picture in your mind, your self-image, and your self-awareness play a big role in whether you will lead morale or sidestep it. More on this later in the chapter on self-awareness.

- They don't know how to lead morale. This book addresses that for sure!

3

Have the courage to be self-aware. Otherwise people won't trust you to be their leader.

CHAPTER THREE

Be Courageously Self-Aware

To lead morale you must know yourself well. Otherwise your pet peeves, fears, and negative thoughts will ooze all over everyone and suffocate morale.

Do you want to be known as an oozer?
It doesn't look good on a resumé!

Lead morale by reducing negativity and igniting can-do attitudes. The key question here is…

Are you strong enough to lead without leaving scars?

> "If people you lead have lost their spark, try looking in the mirror."
> ~*Susan Fowler*

Leaders with inner strength breed success without leaving deep scars. How do they lead morale so successfully?

- They balance purpose/goals with empathy. They focus both on reaching the goals and on respecting the people who must do it. Lean too far in either direction and results or morale suffers.

- They balance humility and self-confidence. Humility respects all. Humility smoothes resistance to change. It elicits contributions. It equalizes. It builds trust. It prevents self-confidence from growing into morale crushing arrogance. Humility serves others.

> "The first responsibility of a leader is to define reality.
> The last is to say thank you. In between the leader is a servant."
> ~*Max DePree, former CEO, Herman Miller*

How do you see humility? Do you see it as weak? If yes, you may be confusing humility for humiliation. Humility is not silence, sheepishness, lack of confidence, or surrender. Humility is open-mindedness not indecisiveness. It elevates everyone's spirit. It elevates the purpose above the personal agenda. It respects all, includes all, and honors diversity. This is its secret power in leading morale.

Conversely, humiliation is a loss of respect and dignity. As a leader, you are more likely to experience humiliation when you do not lead with humility. Ever work for arrogant know-it-all leaders who didn't think anyone else was as valuable as they were? How was your morale? Did you walk around thinking…

WOOPIE! My boss is an arrogant ego-maniac.

Or were you hoping these leaders would fall someday?

On the flip side, have you ever worked with a waffling leader who lacked self-confidence? A leader's lack of confidence and commitment can scar others with abandonment. The key to leading morale is to be confident in your vision and knowledge and humble in delivering it.

- They know and manage their own disappointment and doubts with their inner strength. To lead morale, you must be self-aware and lead yourself to overcome your demons. Your example models how others can do the same.

- They are optimistic realists. They see the reality of challenges and see the possibilities for success. They lead morale with optimism and realism. Lean too much either way and you will lose some of those you lead. Too dreamy-eyed and the realists won't trust you. They will think you are taking them for granted as you overlook the struggles they encounter. Too pessimistic and the optimists will see you as Chicken Little screaming "the sky is falling." Others will follow you into the pessimistic hopeless abyss of negativity. None of this leads high morale.

To lead morale, spread light where there is darkness; don't spread darkness where others need light.

Optimism shines a light to lead everyone from the gray zone into the end zone. Realism prevents the risk of foolish fantasy and denial.

To lead morale, spread light where there is darkness; don't spread darkness where others need light.

- Leaders with inner strength are strong enough to overcome the wonderful comfort of habit. Yet leaders must often lead people out of the status quo, through change, to reach a new level. How do you lead morale during the challenge of change? Certainly not by yielding to the comfort of habit. Acknowledge the challenge but don't encourage resistance.

Ask employees: What talents do we have to succeed in this change? Where have you faced change before and succeeded? People will share stories about relocating, getting married, starting a new career. Connect their individual stories to the strength needed to handle current changes. This highlights their grit and resilience. They overcome the comfort of habit and morale soars.

Self-awareness: What do you believe?

You must also be aware of your leadership beliefs. They shape how you define morale and what you expect of others. They will guide your leadership actions. They will shape how you communicate with your teams and how you respond to their issues.

Leadership Beliefs That Hurt Morale

- **If you can't measure it, it doesn't exist.** This leadership belief, valuable in scientific research, is often misapplied to the business world. First of all, if you apply it to team members' emotional and psychological needs, you will silence people and undermine morale. You may think you are sounding logical, yet you are sounding illogical. What measurements can they use to prove their psychological needs exist? In truth, they will see you as someone who doesn't care as you dismiss their needs for lack of measurable evidence.

  Secondly, if you apply this measurement belief to impending change and demand evidence to guarantee that all changes will work, little will change. Those who don't want the changes will use your measurement belief to block advancement. For those who want change but are afraid to start, you will redouble their fear. Basically, you will not lead change. You will re-secure the status quo. You will not lead morale.

  Picture yourself saying to your team members: "If you can't measure it, it doesn't exist." Will it inspire them to innovate and offer new ideas? Will it encourage them to speak up about team interaction issues that can make or break morale? It's doubtful.

  To lead morale, embrace the truth that many things exist long before people know how to measure them. Listen, observe what's happening, draw on your previous experience, and tap your intuition. Collaborate with the teams to find great solutions. This feeds morale.

  Remember, data can make you feel safe and secure. Overreliance on data blocks innovation and undercuts leading morale.

- **You can't inspire people to do low-level jobs better.** What a ridiculous statement. What a falsehood. What a morale killer!

  Story: A leader asked me to help him address the customer service team's low morale and poor customer service. I assured him that I would inspire and train the team members to deliver high-quality professional customer service. He replied, "Well I don't think anyone would ever consider customer service a profession. I certainly wouldn't." In that one moment, he revealed the core of the low morale problem—his beliefs. If leaders don't value and honor all the work being done, they won't lead morale nor inspire excellence.

■ **There is no "I" in team.** This old chestnut worked well when leadership was all about telling and directing and when work was about sacrifice. This belief tapped into social values of the Silent Generation of WWII and the Baby Boomers they raised. Life and work were about duty and sacrifice. The focus was not on individual talents and needs. It was on collective output. Today employees are inspired by what they each contribute. They see many individual talents that comprise a team.

> Today, employees are inspired by what they *each* contribute.

To lead morale, honor and appreciate individual talents and call on them to contribute to the whole team. More on this later.

Are you fooling yourself—and undermining morale?

Assess the lies you may be telling yourself. Here are some of the most damaging morale-killing lies that leaders bequeath to their teams.

I hired and tolerate the arrogant employee because I can be up front with them. A leader actually said this to me about an arrogant team leader I will call Rodney. Rodney's arrogance was crushing team morale and the leader was doing nothing to stop it. In fact, the entire organization labeled Rodney and the bad morale as "the Rodney effect." Still the leader did nothing. Eventually team members lost respect for the leader. They believed she was a weak leader who couldn't admit her mistake of making Rodney a team leader. Others felt that her lack of action meant she approved of Rodney's behavior. They didn't buy her statement about tolerating Rodney because she could be upfront with him. In their eyes, leaders can be upfront with everyone. They believed she was lying to herself and shirking her responsibilities.

I give people endless chances to develop good attitudes and positive behaviors because I am kind. A leader, whom I will call Tom, made this claim while team members suffered under the continued bad behaviors of a team member I will call Lisa. Teammate after teammate asked him to address the situation. Tom always found reasons to sidestep their requests. Each time, he noted the things Lisa had achieved, claiming nobody is perfect. In the end, the teammates felt that the leader abandoned his responsibility, their well-being, and the positive morale of the workplace. Several left because of Lisa and because of Tom's inaction.

> **Firing people doesn't mean you lack integrity.**

I won't fire people because I have integrity. Firing people doesn't mean you lack integrity and not firing them doesn't mean you have it. Few if any leaders enjoy firing people. Yet if you must let someone go, be honest. Respectfully communicate the reasons and then follow through. Running from your leadership responsibilities leaves a void where morale tumbles.

I can't lead change because you can't change people. You may be fooling yourself but not others. You are telling them you a) don't believe in the change or b) are highly change resistant or c) don't know how to lead change and don't care to learn. If you don't lead change, you abandon everyone in the chaos of change. You are choosing to lead them into an abyss of bad morale and business failure.

My teams know I appreciate them so I don't have to tell them. Even if you and your teams are psychic, you are still missing the point. Sort of knowing you are appreciated and receiving appreciation are two very different things. Giving and receiving appreciation sustains morale like a rechargeable battery. Assuming your teams know you appreciate them drains the morale battery and hides the charger.

Extroverts don't think things through or introverts slow success. These polar views—quite untrue—chill morale and push introverts and extroverts away from each other. Extroverts and introverts work differently toward the same goal. Embrace the differences and tap everyone's talents in order to lead morale.

Checklist: Are you excluding or celebrating diversity?

☐ **Do you grow impatient with people whose personality type is very different from yours?** Do you sideline them and avoid interaction? Or do you acknowledge and honor the differences through communication?

☐ **Do you hire employees that are like you or like the ones you already have on staff?** Some leaders tell themselves that this sameness keeps morale high. Yet it can create a culture that is intolerant of differences. When differences ultimately emerge, and they will, people won't know how to embrace them easily. Morale suffers when people conflict over differences instead of unifying in diverse talents. This is very unfortunate. Team members meet challenges better through broader views and diverse talents—though they may take a bit longer to initially gel as a team.

☐ **Do you actively seek other's views or always state yours first?** If you state your thoughts far more often than you ask for other's ideas, people may see you as having a bias for your own ideas. This disengages and reduces morale. Engage employees and elicit their contributions in order to lead morale.

☐ **Do you react defensively and dig in your heels when people disagree with you?** Anyone can have a moment of defensiveness. However if you do this frequently, your message to others is, "I'm right, you're wrong." This is a morale killer. Be the model of listening, understanding, and discussing different views. These actions don't mean you agree. They don't mean you are weak or indecisive. They mean you sincerely want and consider other's input. This sustains morale.

☐ **Do you sometimes make decisions on employee capabilities based on your assumptions and stereotypes?** *She may not be strong enough to handle this or he may not have the sensitivity to handle this.* Your bias against doing things differently or your fear of risk may be controlling your decisions. Your actions will undercut morale as they silently sideline people, their potential, and possibly their career dreams. Discuss and communicate what is needed to achieve any opportunity. Clear communication sustains morale and creates additional self-awareness.

☐ **Do you stick to your inner circle or let others in?** Leaders and organizations with an inner-circle and a closed door are more likely to exclude diverse people and ideas. This crushes morale. It's a leadership bias that has threatened to sink even the biggest companies like IBM. In the early 1990's, morale had sunk to an all-time low as the stock price plummeted and the handwriting was on the wall. Lou Gerstner, the first outsider to lead IBM, had to break through the years and layers of inner-circle thinking to stop IBM from hitting the skids. He succeeded.

As for morale, inner-circle thinking feels good to everyone in the circle, yet it crushes the morale of those it excludes. Get comfortable with change and diversity. It doesn't mean endless discussions and indecision. It taps the talents you already hired and sustains morale.

☐ **Do you often say, *"this is how we do it here?"*** What does that say to employees? No changes allowed? I have all the power? It is a brick wall to diverse thinking and is not valuable. It kills morale and innovation. Model open-mindedness not indecisiveness.

☐ **Do you accept damaging cliques and mislabel them as friendships?** Leaders have an obligation to prevent or reverse hostile workplaces that shut out and isolate diverse people. If you do nothing, those who are shut out will see you as enabling the hostility. Their morale plummets.

To prevent these cliques, initiate discussions on acceptable teamwork behaviors. Discuss what is the difference between friendships and damaging cliques. This addresses a basic component of morale—belonging—mentioned in the introduction. Cliques marginalize and isolate. Friendships are open and inclusive. To lead morale, you must address the issue of damaging cliques. Eliminate them and prevent new ones from forming.

Seek and destroy cliques.

Action Steps to Get Comfortable with Diversity and Inclusion to Lead Morale

- When you find yourself resisting diverse input, ask more questions. You will discover that what seems radically different actually has some common ground with your views.

- List out your assumptions and fears and then try to disprove them. Gather data and examples that show a clearer and more complete picture.

- Look around and see how and where diverse people are working together. See their success.

Lead morale with self-awareness. Myths, hidden assumptions, untruths, and denials are not a success strategy.

Self-Awareness: Are you a strong leader or a harsh leader?

Some leaders come across as harsh not strong. What's the difference? Harsh leaders disdain and demean the person and the idea. Strong leaders communicate respectfully. They respect others even when they disagree on ideas. Strong leads morale; harsh crushes it.

Some new leaders mistakenly act tough and harsh as they try to establish their authority and build their image of leadership strength. They think it will make people respect them. Over time, many new leaders outgrow this approach. Others don't.

This list can help you assess if you have fallen into the trap of being harsh:

- Do you believe you can't be respected and well-liked? This mistaken belief can drive you to overlook feelings, disrespect others, and seem harsh. The truth is you don't need to choose between likeability and respect. You can be respected and well-liked when you show others basic respect. Respect can even breed likeability.

- Do you think that kindness and humility are weaknesses? If yes, you are likely to come across as harsh and insensitive. But remember, this crushes morale.

- Do you believe that all leadership should be military style? Business is different from military scenarios. In the military, leaders are training troops to react quickly in order to survive and thrive under attack. In business, there are many other conditions to consider. Leadership style has to fit the conditions, goals, and people you are leading. Using a traditional military style in today's business environment can hurt business results and morale.

- Do you believe that honesty and diplomacy are opposites? This is a very damaging belief that drives leaders to be harsh instead of strong. These leaders blurt out messages with immature bluntness that blames, shames, and accuses. They leave a trail of scorched earth and low morale. Strong leaders know that civility doesn't weaken the message. It helps others hear it.

- Were you led by a harsh leader? Have you told yourself it toughened you up and you want to do the same for others? Be careful. Everyone is not you. Moreover, harsh leadership undermines morale even if you get short-term results.

- In your everyday life, is harshness your personal brand? This may sound like a strange question yet there are people who pride themselves on being harsh and blunt. They say things like "I don't have a filter yet people trust me because I'm totally authentic." If this is you, your harshness will cripple morale over time. Remember that being authentic it not a license to be rude, disrespectful, and hurtful. Emotional intelligence guides strong leaders to be simultaneously authentic and respectful. This leads the business and specifically, morale.

"Insults aren't badges of authenticity. Profanity doesn't render you authentic. It just proves you're a child."
~*Frank Bruni, New York Times, October 2016*

Consider this: If you were being introduced to speak at your company's all hands meeting, would you want them to introduce you as: "Here is our leader, an emotionally stunted child."

© 2018 Kate Nasser, CAS, Inc.

Do you revere logic and look down on emotion?

Logic is very valuable—so is emotional intelligence. Leaders who place logic on a pedestal above emotional intelligence often disengage employees whose passion is essential to their morale and success. Logic is not infallible nor is it a panacea for every situation.

In leading morale, logic can fail you when:

- You constantly insist on using *your* logic. There are different logic systems, not just one. Claiming you are logical and others aren't, disengages them. You crush morale instead of leading it. When something *seems* illogical, great leaders ask questions before they label it wrong or illogical.

> **Logic is not infallible nor is it a panacea for everything.**

- You use logic instead of or without emotional intelligence. If you are uncomfortable with emotions, you may be tempted to substitute *logical* behavior that minimizes emotions. When an employee is upset about a situation, immediately blurting out "let's look at this logically" can insult the employee. You are saying that their emotion is not valid and it's time to use the valuable step—logic. Even though you haven't directly called them overly sensitive, your response is insensitive and emotionally stunted.

And guess what? They know what you are insinuating and they are thinking not-so-favorable things about you!

But there is good news. Emotional intelligence and logic are not mutually exclusive. Great leaders develop and use both. This leads morale.

- **You use logic as a reason *not* to communicate.** After a mishap or mistake, have you ever said to yourself, "Didn't they know that already? It's just common sense. It's logical." Not only does *common* sense not exist, logic has little value if you don't communicate it. Great leaders communicate with their teams. They don't label their assumptions as logic that everyone should already know.

Are your teams psychic? No? Then for heaven's sake communicate!

© 2018 Kate Nasser, CAS, Inc.

Logic is a tremendous asset. It brings order out of chaos. It diagnoses and solves problems. Yet it becomes a liability to morale when misapplied, skewed, or labeled as the only thing that matters.

Ego Driven Actions That Undercut Morale

Are you inadvertently undermining morale by these ego driven actions?

- Hoarding your knowledge or giving it only to your favorite employees? This screams "I am important; you're not."

- Exerting your experience over other's input? Morale is all about "you matter." Exerting your experience and shutting out others says "I matter."

- Focusing heavily on goals to the exclusion of interaction? When people want to interact to achieve a goal and your focus on goals shuts down interaction, your "I matter" approach brings down morale.

- Asserting your dominance instead of collaborating? Highly directive leaders say they want people to collaborate yet their directive actions contradict their words. This contradiction disengages people and hurts morale.

- Needing to have the last word on everything? This screams "insecure ego." It silences others and hurts morale.

Lead morale with self-confidence to prevent these ego driven actions.

- Open your ears to feedback. Morale increases when the leader's open-mindedness asks and listens to feedback and ideas.

- Serve others. Self-confidence brings you to serve others. Egotism demands that they serve you and applaud how great you are. Consider what Einstein said: "Only a life lived for others is a life worthwhile."

- Fuel your humility for its strong ability to keep you learning and engaging others.

- Honor your employees' efforts and achievements.

- Overcome fear and doubt that would otherwise cripple your ability to inspire and rally others in tough times.

- Respect the differences, learn to love the differences, and find the fit to lead morale.

Inhale confidence, exhale doubt.

~Author unknown

4

*Get comfortable
with emotion
and showing care!*

CHAPTER FOUR

Are You Comfortable With Emotion?

One important part of self-awareness is knowing how you see and deal with emotion. Here is a simple exercise.

Fill in the blank: Emotion in the workplace is _____.

If you completed the sentence with answers like "out of place, waste of time, unproductive, immature, disruptive, dangerous, inappropriate, annoying, scary, etc…", your belief will undercut your ability to lead morale. Employees aren't unfeeling robots. They are human and human beings have emotions.

When negative emotions arise, listen and understand the issue. Empathize and ask for possible solutions. If there is interaction trouble between employees, help them work it out. Don't snap "work it out for yourselves" and then walk away. To the employees you are abandoning them and running away from difficulty.

Picture a leader who is running away.
Would you follow them? Where would you both be going?
To a make-believe conflict-free heaven?

Show employees how to respect emotions and resolve conflict. If they could work it out for themselves without you, they would.
Honor and address these 16 employee emotional needs to lead and sustain morale. Your efforts will lead morale and teach them to do it too.

1. **The Need to Be Heard.** A huge part of leading morale is addressing this emotional need. This is why listening is critical. Instead of overlooking

the need to be heard in order to reach results sooner, listen to lead morale. Sometimes employees need you to listen and they discover solutions themselves. Show them you care enough to listen.

2. **Quiet Listening.** Similar to the need to be heard, is the need for *quiet* listening. Although some employees want two-way conversation, others want you to listen quietly and take in what they are saying. If you have ever given your opinion to employees who are upset and they didn't respond well, you have learned that *quiet* listening is what these folks want. Their questions don't require answers right now. They mostly want to know that someone has heard them. If you think their issue is critical to the team and to results, then follow the quiet listening with discussion about the issues.

3. **Empathy in Good Times and Bad.** Empathy is a very common emotional need. The sense that someone else knows how you feel, is comforting. Don't keep yourself emotionally distant from your employees. Connect with them through empathy. Empathy is the connection *before* the solution. It is the connection to engagement. It gives those in pain a needed boost to work through their struggles. Avoid the trap of thinking that empathy means you agree with them. It doesn't. It means, *you matter, we matter, this matters.* And remember to empathize with employees' happy events as well as their pain. It doesn't weaken your judgment. It shows you know how to engage them for success. Empathy engages and engagement builds morale. If you aren't convinced, consider that major companies like Cisco and Ford Motor Company are including empathy training for managers and leaders. In an article in the Money section of *Time Magazine*, Denver Knicks reports:

"According to the consultancy Development Dimensions International, roughly 20% of employers in the U.S. now offer empathy training for managers, a sizable increase from 10 years ago, reports *The Wall Street Journal*. Listening and responding skills outranked all others in producing the most successful leaders, according to a DDI study of more than 15,000 leaders in 18 countries released earlier this year. The 10 top performing businesses from among the 160 included in The Empathy Business' 'Global Empathy Index' generated 50% more net income per employee than the bottom 10 performers."

4. **Validation.** Unlike those wanting empathy, these folks want to know you agree with them. Quiet listening can enrage them because they seek reinforcement for what they feel. If you truly disagree, do not tell them while they are upset. They won't hear you and you will seem argumentative and unfeeling. In this case validate that you care about them even though you don't agree with them. When they are done venting, discuss their view and the bigger picture.

Invest in empathy!

5. **Individual Acknowledgement That They Matter.** In diversity, people can feel their identities challenged. When leaders acknowledge what each employee brings to the collective team, people see their own value and the value of team diversity. Individual acknowledgement engages everyone's potential and leads morale!

6. **Outrage.** Perhaps the easiest emotional need to see is the desire for outrage. When people express their outrage over being wronged, it is a safe bet that they want you to share their outrage. You don't have to bad mouth those who wronged them just show understanding about how they feel. Reinforce that they matter. Then discuss what happened to them and next steps.

7. **Support.** There are employees who will come to you when they need support. Other employees won't come to ask for support because they fear you will see them as needy and weak. Yet, these folks are *indirectly* asking for support in the care they give you and teammates. They believe their supportive actions speak volumes. They don't understand why you haven't heard them. Get to know your employees. Listen to their words and observe their actions. Give them support and let them know that you don't see asking for help as a weakness.

8. **Encouragement—It Mentors.** If you want employees to innovate, change, and grow, you must encourage them. When they want to ditch the conventional and try something different, encourage them beyond their fear and doubt. Successful leaders encourage growth and kindle positive emotions about it. It leads morale. If whatever employees want to try is too risky, discuss the reasons why and encourage them to explore *other* innovations.

9. **Psychological Safety.** Employees need to know that they can make mistakes as they develop without you pouncing on them and labeling them as inept. Learning through mistakes is the path to employees building a sense of competence—an important psychological need. They also need to know they can raise issues without being labeled difficult and uncooperative. They need to know that it's OK to be themselves vs. being your clone. Any tactics you use that bully, manipulate, punish, and abuse, can undermine psychological safety and dissolve morale.

Do you want to be known as the pouncer?
Or a leader who develops others' greatness?

© 2018 Kate Nasser, CAS, Inc.

Read this first hand story from Achim Nowak, CEO of Brilliant Best Mastermind, as he recounts the high morale in one of his previous low-paying jobs:

After I left my career in showbiz, I was hired as a trainer for the Victim Services Agency in Manhattan. We trained managers and school teachers to become mediators. It was a challenging job and I loved this "good work." In hindsight, I realized that I loved it because morale among this underpaid bunch of trainers was exceptional and that was no lucky accident. Morale was fostered by the fine skill of my boss, Lynne Hurdle-

Price, Director of Mediation Training Division. One of the key steps was a two-hour staff meeting every other Friday. We invariably arrived at these staff meetings tired and cranky and we left buoyed and uplifted. Besides the ice breaker at the beginning of the meeting, we used community guidelines in the meeting on how to engage with each other. These explicit guidelines created a tangible sense of safety within the team that made it fun to engage. Even when we discussed a serious topic, there was a sense of lightness and light that fueled our morale.

10. **Devil's Advocate—Critical View.** Whether it is about their career or an important project, employees sometimes want the benefit of an opposite opinion. These folks see this as essential support. Yet be sure they want this opposing view before giving it; otherwise you may seem like an insensitive oaf.

    Also, don't mislabel their request for an opposing view as lack of self-confidence or incompetence. It takes a strong person to seek opposite views. Ask incisive questions to help them think through the challenge. Your actions support them and lead morale.

    A Personal Example: A friend and I are quite different when it comes to dating. She is more willing to give a boyfriend many chances even when he continues to treat her badly. She had been through two relationships where men treated her badly and both ended in break-ups. On the third bad relationship, she asked me what she should do. Surprised that she would ask me, I said to her "Are you sure you want my opinion?" She chuckled and said, "Yes, I am asking you because I know you'll tell me to drop him." I then gave her my honest opinion. Yet I didn't assume at the beginning that she wanted my views just because she was telling me the problem. I verified what she wanted from me and then offered assistance.

11. **Knowledge—Necessary Data.** There are people who find knowledge a great comfort. They don't want your opinion. They want your knowledge. They want you to share the information and experience that you have, that they don't. Employees with an analytic personality type are especially sustained through knowledge, experience, and logic. They want the data you have. Lead the morale of analytic employees with experienced-based examples, information, and knowledge.

12. **Insight—The Halfway Point.** Employees who want your insight are already moving ahead with a challenge. They want more than knowledge and less than a solution. They want insight. A combination of "maybe statements" and questions are the dynamic duo here. It allows them to work through the current block with the light of your insight. Lead morale by being a conduit to the solution.

13. **Solutions—The Right Way, Not Right Away.** Listen, give empathy, validate what they want. Then offer possible solutions. Many leaders want to offer solutions right away. They think it is logical and productive—the sooner the solution, the sooner the success. Unfortunately, to someone who is not ready for a solution, the "get through it quickly" approach seems disconnected, out-of-touch, and somewhat domineering. Be ready to give empathy and validation before you offer alternatives.

14. **Strength and Confidence—Especially in Tough Times.** When people feel vulnerable—even scared—strength may be the greatest care possible. Strength and confidence reduce fear. This is frequently the case during times of uncertainty and confusion like during organizational change. Your strength of purpose and conviction give them a sense of certainty and control. Your strength buoys them and emboldens them to deal with the challenge. Give your strength without judging them. Judging makes employees feel weaker. Your strength and confidence make them feel stronger.

Share the spotlight!

15. **Credit—Share the Spotlight.** Achievement and accomplishments spur additional contributions and commitment. Employees need to know their work is appreciated. Share the spotlight. Recognize individual talents and how they contribute to the whole. Offer your gratitude. It doesn't create divas. It ignites more contribution.

16. **Momentum—Transfer of Energy.** If you are seen as action-oriented, employees may come to you to ride the wave of your momentum and move forward. It takes practice to spot how much momentum they want. Are they coming to you for a little boost or a rocket launch? When companies bring me in to (as they call it) light a fire in their employees, I ask, *how hot a fire?*

Until you learn how to spot how strong a push employees want, ask them how much they want. It's simple to do and it shares responsibility.

Leading morale means energizing employees at the right moment with the right amount of momentum. If you misstep, push too hard and demoralize them, apologize. Better to boost their morale again than wrongly accuse them of dragging their feet. This moment is about their success not about your ego.

Honoring all of these emotions will help you mentor and promote more diverse people into leadership. If you continue to believe that emotion in the workplace is inappropriate or bad, you might select less-feeling employees for leadership positions and foster a cold heartless culture.

Caring words cost nothing. They create infinite possibilities and sustain morale. Don't mistake caring words as weak, risky, or beating around the bush. Their power comes in what they do and don't do.

Caring words...

- Build trust.

- Develop relationships between strangers.

- Open closed minds with empathy and trust.

- Strengthen relationships to ride through rough storms together.

Caring words don't...

- Create scars or rip open old wounds.

- Trigger defensiveness that slows down success.

- Create resentment that overshadows the true business purpose.

- Build walls that block collaboration and future opportunities.

Caring words are emotional intelligence in action.

- They are based on respect for all humans even in disagreement.

- They require a positive self-image that doesn't preach to others.

- They are the courageous choice to "give before you receive."

By honoring employee emotions and using caring words, you become a buoy of morale. Notice I didn't say THE buoy of morale. The goal isn't dependence on you. The goal is to model it and so everyone can buoy morale.

- **Share your inspiration.** Don't withhold your inspiration thinking that withholding it will build employees' independence.

- **Show respect to buoy respect.** Basic human respect is a buoyant force. Without it, teams sink. Great leaders show respect to everyone. Respect keeps everyone afloat in rough currents. It doesn't coddle and weaken them as some harsh leaders like to think.

- **Share positive emotion.** Kudos, appreciation, and a can-do mindset teach everyone how to buoy morale. Pessimists believe that this is sugar coating. They think it is dreamy optimism that denies the truth and can lead to business failure. Not true. A positive attitude doesn't rewrite the truth. It spotlights the true positives that help everyone get through the tough moments. Be a buoy to sustain all in tough times.

- **Build inspiration as the culture.** Whatever behaviors people repeat become the culture. To lead morale practice positive behaviors daily. Learning (not blaming) creates a learning culture. Engaging (not telling) creates a empowered culture. Responsibility (not selfishness) creates a culture of contribution and shared leadership. Daily doses of inspiration vs. a 'just get-to-work' approach creates a positive can-do culture.

- **Be flexible and celebrate flexibility.** One of the most maddening aspects of tough times is having to abandon one project/product to develop another. Committed team members feel a loss of what they didn't complete. They can feel demoralized and lose energy and productivity. Leaders can minimize and even prevent this effect. Be a model of flexibility. It keeps productivity afloat in times of change.

- **Play along the way.** Driver personality types find tough challenges energizing and highly motivating. This isn't true of every personality type on the team. To some, tough challenges feel like struggle. They need fun times to sustain morale for the tough times. Great leaders lead morale by including play along the way.

Action Checklist

Do you lead morale through appreciation? Or do you pull people down because:

☐ You are very uncomfortable expressing positive emotion.

☐ You were mentored by leaders who thought emotion was unproductive so that's how you lead.

☐ The culture of the organization is not one of gratitude so you follow suit.

☐ You live by the old rule: No news is good news. You think employees are paid to do a job and their morale is their responsibility.

☐ You believe that they know they are appreciated because they were hired.

☐ You are an introvert who keeps much inside and sharing your inspiration is tiring.

☐ Your leader doesn't express appreciation to you and so you don't show it to your team members.

Be a buoy of inspiration and balance.

☐ You are intrinsically motivated and need little appreciation. You assume employees are like you.

☐ You are a high driver personality focusing on end results not on showing appreciation.

If you answered yes to any of these above, re-read the section in this chapter that applies to your challenge. Your behavior change will lead morale.

5

*Be courteous.
It communicates the
most basic element
of morale—respect.*

CHAPTER FIVE

Use the Power of Courtesy and Communication

Comfort with positive emotion gives you access to one very powerful yet simple tool for leading morale—courtesy!

Many mislabel courtesy as political correctness and being vague. It isn't. Courtesy is respect in action and is THE cost free way to lead morale. Courtesy is considering another's need for respect as you communicate and interact.

9 Point Courtesy Checklist to Lead Morale Every Single Day

1. **Greet politely and warmly.** Welcome new teammates on their first day. Introduce them and have the team actively engage them. This addresses the human need to connect and belong. It sets teamwork in motion and elevates morale. Greet and engage employees at the beginning of a meeting to overcome typical meeting apathy. This leads morale.

2. **Start a request with please.** It was everywhere in decades past. Has it slipped away? Grab hold of it and put it back in every request. This one small word communicates respect that prevents others from misconstruing your request as an order. To lead morale, this is essential.

3. **Give sincere and abundant thank yous.** The gift of gratitude is free yet far from cheap. People hold gratitude in high regard. It is quite dear. Moreover, a leader's appreciation goes far beyond individual thank yous. It creates a culture of gratitude that sustains employee morale. Leaders who lead morale put gratitude on everyone's courtesy checklist.

> "It's not what gets ranked, it's what gets thanked."
> ~*Sheila Heen, The Global Leadership Summit*

4. **Interact with an open mind.** Open-mindedness is a part of courtesy. It considers other's needs and views and eases interaction. To lead morale welcome employees ideas and contributions with an open mind. Solutions and success come from openness.

5. **Use good manners.** There are habits that most people consider rude: talking too loud, slurping drinks, smacking lips when eating, clinking utensils, eating while you're on the phone, going through a door and not holding it for the next person behind you, not saying hello when you enter a room. Sustained rude behavior signals disregard for others. When a leader is rude and uses bad manners most or all of the time, morale slips.

6. **Show interest but don't pry.** Asking teammates about their weekend can start the week off well. Grilling them with personal questions feels intrusive and can build walls that hurt morale and success. Likewise, showing interest in customers is a courtesy that warms the relationship. Prying into their lives can slam the door shut.

7. **Share information. Don't gossip.** Communicating information is critical to leading morale. Gossiping can kill it. Gossip is rooted in assumptions that destroy trust and teamwork.

8. **Don't generalize.** Generalizations about people will assuredly disrespect someone. One day, I heard an employee state that people who work in government are lazy. He didn't consider that his co-workers had friends and family who worked in the public sector. Besides making himself look like a bigot, his discourteous remark marred his work relationships and teamwork. Don't generalize about people. Respect individuality and diversity to lead morale.

9. **Smile, don't snicker or smirk.** Non-verbal communication impacts morale. Positive body language uplifts and engages. Negative body language ranges from rude to derisive. When it becomes derisive, it demeans others. In its extreme form, like mimicking and mocking

people's behaviors or traits, it constitutes bullying. Negative body language and treating people badly push people away. Respectful positive behavior like courtesy draws people in and leads morale.

Courtesy never goes out of fashion. It feels great to receive it. In business, it's more than a nicety. Courtesy opens doors, impresses in first meetings, shows respect, expresses care, smooths rough moments, defuses tension, bridges gaps, and leads morale.

Honesty with courtesy leads morale. Bluntness (rough emotion-packed honesty) squashes morale. Honesty with courtesy is one choice in communicating. Bluntness is another. Bluntness squashes morale; courtesy with honesty elevates it.

Honesty can hurt but blunt burns forever with emotional scars. Honesty delivered with courtesy maintains an air of respect. Blunt criticism triggers defensive reactions that block great morale. Without the emotion of bluntness, employees can clearly hear an honest courteous message. Civility and courtesy don't weaken your message. They help others to hear it and embrace it.

> **Honesty with courtesy leads morale. Bluntness bombs out.**

6 Logical Reasons That Bluntness Bombs Out

- **No Warm-Up.** Picture your bluntness as very cold water. If you push someone into a cold swimming pool, they first have to deal with the shock. They may even remember the shock and focus on it. If you want people to hear and embrace your message, don't shock them with bluntness. Use honesty with courtesy to help them wade into the pool and adjust to what you're saying.

- **Punching Dulls the Brain.** Punching bags are not known for their performance. They hang and swing. If you deliver a blunt verbal punch, those you verbally punch may swing back at you or away from you. They are not likely to understand your deeper message nor change their behavior.

- **Bluntness builds barriers.** People communicate in order to connect. Your bluntness can create a busy signal blocking the connection. It is a barrier between you and those you are speaking to. Since they can't hear you, your message essentially bombs out.

- **Bluntness undermines respect and credibility.** The roughness of the approach can weaken the strength of your message. Who is going to respect and believe your message if you come across as an insensitive oaf? They will focus on how poorly you communicate not on your message.

- **Bluntness breaks bonds.** Most people aren't hermits. They interact and build bonds with others to survive and thrive. Bluntness may get your words out but it bombs out by breaking important bonds. It may even create vengeful feelings and start a verbal war.

- **Bluntness focuses on your needs and overlooks others.** Bluntness screams selfishness. It lacks emotional intelligence. It's no wonder that bluntness turns others off.

Don't assume it's OK to be blunt. Bluntness is based on trust and must be invited not offered. When people have built loads of trust and respect is high, sometimes bluntness is accepted. This is why you often see bluntness among leaders and teams that have worked together for years and years. They have built the trust needed to remove the sting of bluntness.

7 Steps to Go From Brutally Blunt to Helpfully Honest

1. **Honor people as well as your message.** Most bluntness is driven by your needs and the *singular focus on what you want* to communicate. That's how it creates trouble. Honor others as well as your message.

2. **Be open to other possibilities.** What you say is rarely an absolute fact. There are other perspectives, conditions, opinions, and possibilities to consider. When you communicate from this mindset, you are more likely to have an honest dialogue with people instead of a blunt monologue. Stay open to other views to avoid being blunt.

3. **In difficult situations, never start a sentence with the word you.** Imagine saying, "You aren't doing your job" or "You are failing badly." Starting with "you" comes across as a blunt attack. It dings morale and breeds a defensive response. Instead, start with "Here's what we need

and this is what we see you doing. Let's talk about how you see it and how to close the gaps." Now the employee can hear your message and you can discuss specifics on what to change.

4. **Separate the emotion out of negative situations to avoid being brutally blunt.** Say, "I want to put aside my emotion and talk about this situation." It shows the other person you want to speak honestly without insulting them. However, do not use this intro to justify being blunt. It's hypocritical. Your words and actions must honor people with honesty rather than bruise them with bluntness.

5. **Use a sense of proportion to reduce bluntness.** Bluntness, by definition, is the negative extreme of communication. Bluntness is emotion packed. Ask yourself: Why must I use this extreme and inflict scars? What words, with better proportion, can clearly communicate my message?

6. **Develop a sense of timing and watch your tone of voice.** Most everyone accepts the value of a positive tone of voice. Yet when some people read the word *timing*, they assume it means delay. Timing doesn't always mean delay. There are times you can't or shouldn't delay a conversation. However, timing can also mean the pace of your speech. The faster you speak in tough moments, the more brutal it sounds. Meanwhile, speaking too slowly or softly can sound patronizing. A normal even pace of speech communicates honesty and avoids bluntness. This leads and sustains morale.

7. **Think agreement.** Thinking about finding common ground reduces your bluntness. Replace negative emotion with positive desire. Ask for what you want instead of railing on about what you don't want. It transforms your communication from hurtful and blunt to honest and positive. Helpful honesty produces a yes; insults rarely do. Even if agreement is not your goal, think "yes" and your words will be helpfully honest vs. brutally blunt.

The question people often ask me: Are there people with whom you must be brutally blunt? No. I have met people who don't understand subtle communication. In those moments, I am much more direct but not brutally blunt. There is a big difference! I still show them respect and courtesy while I get to the point sooner and with more direct language. Respect is the key to being honest instead of blunt. It honors people as well as your message. If you disagree, state your view with calmness and respect for others.

To be clear, courtesy doesn't mean lack of honesty. They go hand in hand in sustaining morale. Conversely, bluntness and lack of honesty both erode trust and morale.

Passive aggressive leaders reduce trust as they confuse and frustrate employees. Most employees want leaders to say what they mean and mean what they say. Yet how can leaders do this without being blunt, derisive, rude, and disrespectful? Once again the answer is sincere honesty delivered with civility. It shows courage, humility, and respect. Anyone can selfishly blast out their candor. That is immature weak-willed bullying which erodes morale. Few people want that nor respond well to it.

> *Lead with sincerity not power!*
> *It draws everyone in. It energizes thought,*
> *engagement, contribution, and morale.*

Prepare what you want to say with honesty and deliver with courtesy and civility. Honesty is what you say and civility is how you say it. Civility doesn't weaken the authenticity of the message. It helps everyone hear it with less resistance. Since people don't feel insulted or attacked, they listen to your message vs. trying to deflect it or escape it.

Be confident in your message and humble in delivering it. Humility and civility make tough honesty palatable. They lead and sustain morale.

Example: I had to remind a people skills online community member not to post messages on the community page selling her company's products and services. I explained the guideline, the reason, and suggested she do as I do—place product information on her own social media page. I took this approach instead of blasting her with a rough warning message. I was honest in a civil way instead of attacking her with brutal bluntness. She agreed to the guideline and stayed in the community.

Reach 'em; don't preach 'em. Before you speak, ask yourself if you are preaching to employees or reaching them. Preaching has the sub-message, "I know more than you do." Reaching them respects other's knowledge while communicating honestly. If you're not sure which way you come across, ask for feedback. Also watch how often you deliver negative messages vs. positive ones. If you communicate the negative far more often, you may be preaching your individual view. Leadership and leading morale are about the big picture not purely about what troubles you right now.

Rise above your personal preferences. It lessens the mini-me syndrome where you expect everyone to be like you. It honors diversity and boosts morale. To do it, become very self-aware. Know your personality type, your learning style, and your ability to change and adapt. Practice being adaptable every single day. It prevents you from falling into domineering self-absorption. This leads morale.

> **Reach 'em; don't preach 'em.**

Be likeable without constantly seeking to be liked. Be likeable by delivering every message—even the tough ones—with civility. Don't avoid conflict just to be liked. If you seek to be liked at every moment, you may avoid necessary conversations. This can anger employees who must endlessly tolerate bad situations that you won't address. For example, if there is an employee with a very bad attitude and negative behaviors, address this with honesty, civility, courage, respect, and clarity.

Separate facts from feelings. Your candor has feelings in it that are masquerading as facts. As a result, it can insult and disrespect others. Use honesty instead. Unlike candor, honesty separates facts from feelings.

> **Seeking to be liked at every moment can actually kill morale!**

For example, when an employee complains constantly, your candid response "stop whining" communicates your emotion. It is patronizing, derisive, and disrespectful. Instead, tell them honestly that you welcome their suggested improvements beyond the complaints.

Moreover, "stop whining" is also in and of itself, a whine! It's a complaint about what you don't like disguised as an order. If you want to break the pattern, model the behavior you want to see from them. Ask the employee, who constantly complains, for some solutions. If that is not feasible, simply state the facts about what can and cannot change. It's authentic not offensive. You lead morale by modeling what to do vs. declaring what not to do.

6

*Address chronic
complaining and
stop negativity from
planting its roots.*

CHAPTER SIX

Address Chronic Complaining and Negativity

Chronic complaining and negativity can undermine morale and create a low morale culture. To lead morale, address chronic complainers. In Dr. Robert Sutton's book, Good Boss, Bad Boss, he notes: "Teams with downers produce 40-60% less than teams without them." That certainly rang true to me.

When I consult to teams with chronic complainers, I sometimes feel like I'm pushing a truck up a hill without a motor.

Have you ever felt that way?

> *Chronic complaining drags positive into negative*
> *and undermines morale and performance.*

Ways to respond to chronic faultfinders and complainers:

1. **Heighten their awareness.** Are they aware that they come across as negative? You might think this is a ridiculous question yet many people never think about how they appear to others. If someone is going to change their own behavior, first they must see how their behavior comes across to others and how it impacts everyone. Heighten their awareness through honest courteous discussions.

2. **Use the power of the written "what if".** Your goal here is to get them to generate solutions not just complaints. Ask everyone in a meeting to *write down* some possible solutions for a current problem. "What if we _____." Now go around the room and have each person share aloud the possible solutions they wrote down. The *written mechanism* casts a stronger spotlight on solutions. The chronic faultfinders will see their behavior more clearly if they have nothing to contribute to the discussion when it is their turn to speak. By going to the written form, you create a verbal stream of possible solutions that can outshine apathetic silence and endless complaints.

3. **If the chronic faultfinding continues, ask them "What does faultfinding do for you or mean to you?"** This question asks without accusing. If they are finding fault with ideas without offering new ones, they are resisting change. If they are always finding fault in people, it shows their personal fears and insecurities. In either case, discussing their faultfinding can get them to move past it. As a consultant, I've initiated these discussions and helped many become positive contributors. To lead morale, sometimes you have to dig deep to uncover the obstacles.

4. **Take what is valuable. Set limits on the rest.** If they are highlighting valid risks or flaws in an idea, reinforce those points and ask them what alternatives do they see. Sometimes faultfinders create solutions once you have validated their critical eye. However, if they are finding fault in you and other employees as people, set limits appropriately: "I treat you with respect. I expect and request the same for me and everyone here."

Chronic faultfinding and complaining comes from fear, selfishness, and low emotional intelligence. Counteract the powerful draw of negativity with your self-confidence, optimism, and emotional intelligence. When you address negativity, you lead morale.

Many people are drawn to negativity because it makes them feel:

- Protected and secure. It keeps them on guard and ready to survive the inevitable trouble that they think life presents.

- Validated for past pain they have suffered and still feel.

- Powerful instead of powerless.

- At ease. Thinking that work and life are bad is easier than thinking they could make it better.

Chronic negativity, complaining, and faultfinding feel safe. To counteract this and lead morale, make it as safe to find solutions as it is to complain.

1. **Replace your unstated expectations with communication. To lead morale, don't get stuck in your own silent expectations.** If you find yourself thinking, *employees should stop complaining*, then get busy. Elicit their ideas and solutions. It gets you out of yourself and into leading morale with them.

2. **Politely interrupt the negative to ask for the positive.** The best way to teach behavior is to model it and ask others to do it. When chronic complainers dump their doubts on everyone, ask them for one way to make the situation better. If they complain some more, politely interrupt them and say, "I heard what you don't like. How can we fix it?" Consistently break through the complaint with a sincere request for ideas. It sends a consistent and strong message that leads morale.

3. **Applaud initiative not just success.** To lead morale honor people who initiate ideas and solutions. Give them recognition for showing initiative. Highlight why initiative matters. This is not the same thing as rewarding end results and success. If you want less complaining, recognize, appreciate, and reward initiative as well as results and success.

4. **Discuss what is *and* is not working**. Many leaders focus only on what is not working. They believe it increases efficiency and speeds success.

In an employee engagement workshop that I was leading, the manager's boss surprised us and suddenly joined the session. As the employees started outlining what was going well, the leader blurted out, *"Why are we wasting time on what we've done well? Let's move on to what isn't working."* BAM. You could feel the energy plummet. His message doused morale instead of igniting it.

Focusing purely on what's not working creates a culture of chronic negativity and complaining. If employees don't hear positive feedback for the solutions they've created, why would they continue to be solution-focused? Applaud positive attitudes/efforts and celebrate progress.

5. **Acknowledge the emotion; don't encourage it.** Chronic negativity can become white noise that people see as normal and unavoidable. They begin to tolerate it. It can become the culture. Yet this is death to morale.

> **Leading morale requires celebrating progress to keep progress going.**

Acknowledge the emotions that are creating negativity and then engage employees in positive solutions. Don't participate in the negativity because it encourages everyone to perpetuate it. Emotional intelligence guru Daniel Goleman goes even further than this and encourages leaders to practice a positive outlook by a) being aware of your outlook, b) redirecting your mind to something positive in the moment and c) considering positive interpretations of what felt negative. "Being skilled at seeing the positive, even in adverse situations, is one aspect of emotional intelligence that distinguishes high performing leaders." I would add that high performing leaders lead morale through the positive not the negative.

6. **Correct yourself out loud when you lapse into complaining.** Anyone can complain. When you slip into it, stop yourself. Illustrate how you turn around your own behavior. Model this turnaround for everyone. It builds respect and leads morale.

7. **Park your ego and elevate your self-confidence.** Trust that your position as leader is strengthened when you welcome and recognize employee talents, ideas, solutions, and contributions. This shows your self-confidence as a leader. If you are insecure when others shine, you will squash contribution and morale.

8. **Educate them on the bigger business picture and help them discover their value.** Un-empowered employees who think they don't matter to the business show their frustration through negativity. Share the bigger picture so they can see how they belong and contribute.

> **Park your ego and elevate your self-confidence.**

Example: A technical support desk in a large healthcare hospital system had poor morale and performance. The uninspired employees complained about how many calls they had, the customers' attitudes, and the stress. The leader began rotating the tech support analysts out into the hospital and medical offices to see the bigger picture. They saw how technical problems impacted healthcare workers and patients. Now they could see directly how their problem solving work made a difference. This transformed the tech support analysts' attitudes and behaviors. It transformed morale.

9. **Share power and responsibility.** I've seen great leaders turn chronic complainers into star performers. These leaders give the complainers true responsibility to be accountable for results. This change creates a new reality for the complainers. Chronic complaining no longer serves them. Responsibility evokes new behavior and eventually a change in their self-images. They see themselves as people who actively create solutions vs. passively complain.

Conversely, if you are a micro-manager or a highly controlling leader, you breed discontent. Employees feel you don't need their insight, talent, or skills. They feel they have no value nor power. Addressing this means empowering not delegating. Delegating tells them you still have the power. Empowering them shares power and shows them they have the ability and responsibility to make a difference and be accountable.

Delegating instead of empowering is a frequent mistake I see leaders make in trying to lead morale. They think delegating will engage employees and boost morale. It doesn't. Delegation says: *do these things, follow the rules, and report back.*

Check your beliefs about empowerment and employee engagement. One leadership team realized that they believed employees had to *earn the right* to engage and offer ideas. They reached out only to top performers and overlooked everyone else.

As we worked through their beliefs, they realized that employee engagement is not a reward you give to top performers. Employee engagement is how you foster top performance. It's how you get fewer complaints and more actionable ideas. It's how you lead morale.

Empower and engage. It reduces negativity and prevents gripe fests and chronic complaining. It becomes a culture that balances emotion with productivity—a culture of high morale.

**Empower employees—including the chronic complainers—
to ignite their positive contributions!**

© 2018 Kate Nasser, CAS, Inc.

7

*Replace blame
with accountability.
Blame kills morale.
Accountability sustains it.*

CHAPTER SEVEN

Breed Accountability, Not Blame

A culture of high morale and productivity hinges on leading for accountability not blame. Accountability is the practice of initiative, ownership, and follow-through. It benefits morale and the financial success of the organization. Accountability doesn't come from blame and is not the same as blame.

Blame...

- Encourages people to avoid initiative and responsibility.

- Turns high function into dysfunction.

- Pumps up politics (who's liked/disliked) and deflates morale.

- Disengages employees in order to self-protect and self-preserve.

- Wastes time that could be spent on positive steps.

- Kills all hope of initiative.

While you are leading *blame*, accountable leaders and teams with great morale are...

- Learning, repairing, rebuilding, and solving

- Innovating over new challenges

- Valuing and tapping everyone's talent

- Expanding insights and knowledge

- Collaborating for success

- Growing the business and developing the talent

- Farming new business territory

- Wowing each customer

- Producing profits

If you become the leader of a demoralized organization that was previously focused on blame, what can you do to lead morale now?

- Communicate the new vision of accountability without blaming the previous blame-focused leader.

For high morale and productivity, breed accountability, not blame.

- Promote participation. Encourage ideas. Show them that you welcome and value ideas and recognize contribution. It's a big hurdle of trust for employees to climb yet they can do it. I have helped leaders and teams do exactly this.

- Meet individually with employees and hear their perspectives. You gain a wealth of information about your employees and the big picture of the morale challenges. Listening to them begins to build trust.

- Do workplace sessions that focus on learning about everyone's talents and showing appreciation for initiative and contribution. It builds trust. With highly mistrustful demoralized teams, do not start with the team building activity known as the trust fall. Trust building in a demoralized organization takes time. Jumping into the ultimate test of trust—the trust fall—comes across as an insensitive mandate.

- Empower them to hold you accountable. One of the best ways to teach the difference between accountability and blame is to ask them to hold you accountable for your promises.

- To convert a culture of blame to one of high morale and accountability, lead with a passion for learning. Everyone makes mistakes. Blaming cultures label people as inept. Accountable cultures focus on learning and the responsibility to apply what you learn.

As you eliminate the vestiges of blame, resentment, and fear, you free the employees to be accountable for success. You will witness improved communication and collaboration that bring about shared ownership. You will see morale soar as scapegoating, blame, and resentment disappear.

Remember, nothing productive comes from resentment. "Resentment is weak and lowers self-esteem." ~Barbara Sher, Best selling author of seven books on goal achievement.

> **A culture of learning transforms blame into accountability and growth.**

Moreover, if you see other interaction difficulties, lead morale by facilitating better interaction. Leaders who mislabel poor interaction as just personality conflicts:

- create a greater divide among team members.

- drive people to be silent to protect themselves from your dismissive remarks about personality conflicts.

- weaken core values of respect, honesty, communication, truth, and accountability.

Discover what the trouble is; don't assume what it is.

Leading morale means encouraging respectful open communication for great collaboration. Don't gloss over interaction trouble.

Trying to keep the peace can keep you from finding the peace.

Initiate and invite discussion on these potential trouble spots for morale:

- Positive behaviors for shared work spaces

- Productive behaviors for meetings including arrival, texting, listening, interjecting, etc…

- Acceptable ways to disagree and discuss strong views

- Aggressive and passive aggressive behavior

- Constant negativity and extreme pessimism

- Self-absorbed, demanding, entitled, maverick behaviors

In these discussions work with all the employees to create a clear list of behaviors that define a great attitude. A great attitude is essential not negotiable. Everyone must have it and live it.

In teamwork, great attitudes fuel momentum. Bad attitudes destroy good ones, as well as destroying momentum and morale. In customer service, great attitudes draw customers back to your organization. Bad attitudes destroy revenue, customer loyalty, and even the brand. In leadership, great attitudes empower and honor employees. Bad attitudes create a toxic culture that crushes morale.

By defining what behaviors correspond to a great attitude, you reduce interaction difficulties through clarification and consensus. For everyone to be accountable for how they behave, they must first discuss how they impact each other. Knowledge empowers people to be accountable for their actions. Otherwise, they defend themselves with statements like, "I didn't know that bothered you" or blame others with remarks like, "You are too sensitive."

Breed accountability and you foster great morale.

Model great morale. Discuss it, encourage it, and facilitate it. Positive inspiration can overcome negative tendencies and habits.

8

*Highlight
individual talents.
It says "you matter."
It spurs contribution.
It heightens morale.*

CHAPTER EIGHT

Highlight Individual Talents

Now it's time to take accountability to the next level by highlighting people's talents. When you show employees how you and the organization value their talents, their contributions and accountability can soar.

To lead morale, honor individual talents and show how they contribute to the whole. Invite people to use them fully. This inspires positive attitudes, initiative, and accountability.

The challenge for some leaders is that they are not sure what talents to identify. Here is a list of 25 to honor, celebrate, and appreciate. Who in your organization is…

1. **A great collaborator.** Those who have natural collaboration skills or have developed them through years of work are a definite asset to any team.

2. **A memory bank.** Even the greatest computers don't replace someone with a memory for BOTH what has transpired and the *human impact and reaction to it*. The memory banks on your team become the team's intuition and collective gut for in-the-moment decisions.

3. **A motivator.** Those who inspire themselves and others to higher levels bring every organization to unimagined success.

4. **A velvet truth teller.** These people are naturally good at speaking the truth with care not bluntly and brutally. They deliver the truth without squashing respect and trust.

5. **A creative.** Having a creative on a team whose function is not primarily creative expands the team's capacity to work on non-standard requests and its ability to work with creative departments. Find the creatives in your organization.

6. **An innovator.** Those who love innovation and initiate it fuel evolution. They prevent the failure that comes from inertia and resistance to change. They bring a mindset of continuous improvement.

7. **A supporter.** Supporters naturally anticipate needs, willingly fill gaps, and often excel at last minute problem solving. This is valuable for every organization.

8. **An empathizer.** Teamwork needs more than occupational skills to succeed. It needs people with emotional intelligence who can sustain each other. An empathizer does this naturally, easily, and well. Empathizers help all to rise above tough times to reach the goals.

9. **A sounding board.** They know exactly when to observe, when to listen, and when to question. They uplift all who experience this gift.

10. **A get-it-done teammate.** Without action, ideas die. These champions of follow-through drive home success.

11. **A healthy skeptic.** Healthy skeptics challenge assumptions and prevent groupthink to keep progress flowing. Unlike pessimists, they don't drown everyone in negativity.

12. **A critical thinker.** They always see the crucial issues clearly even amid noise and confusion. Their critical thinking value is undisputed. Organizations often tap them for leadership positions yet they are not always interested in being leaders. Honor their critical thinking.

13. **A port in a storm.** Those who can keep the calm for themselves and others during unexpected chaos keep the teams balanced and performing well during the tumultuous times.

14. **A practical philosopher.** Philosophical insights can sustain morale, move people beyond obstacles, and even solve problems. With their broader view, these practical philosophers see solutions that others overlook.

15. **A balance beam.** These employees see both sides of every issue. They easily give and take. They have hope yet still understand despair. They love the present and adapt easily to the future. Balance beams become the solid base of success for the organization. They aren't neutral. They are balanced engines moving everyone forward!

16. **A sprinter.** Bursts of winning energy help teams handle sudden changes and requests, jump the hurdles, and win the day.

17. **A marathoner.** Picture a grueling project that is not a sprint. Marathoners are an endless pump of energy, hope, and action during the long haul.

18. **A billboard of diversity.** Employees of mixed culture or race, or those who have lived in different countries, grew up with parents of different generations, etc... bring a valuable spark of open-mindedness and insight to the organization.

19. **A mix of personality types.** Personality type differences can often be the source of discord. People who are on the border of different personality types help smooth the rough edges and blend the diversity into success.

20. **A double cookie.** This is a phrase I coined for people who have great capacity to use their left and right brains together. Instead of being heavily analytic left brain *or* tipping all the way over to the creative right side, double cookies deliver the power of creative analysis and the big picture. They can spot when the team is trapped on either side or in a war between the two sides. They show the team the intersection of both sides.

21. **An intuitive.** Historically, workplace cultures have marginalized the value of intuition. That is slowly changing and teams are embracing the talent of intuition that speeds success. If you are leading a technical organization that has trouble moving from data to decisions, bring an intuitive onto the team to undo the paralysis.

22. **An organizer.** The natural organizer clears the road of complexity for all to reach success.

23. **A transplant.** Employees who have worked in many industries, or professions, or even departments in the organization deliver the single greatest advantage to reducing silos. Don't label them as unreliable because they moved around. Benefit from their broad experience.

24. **A rainmaker.** This rare ability to create opportunities and attract new customers is not just for sales departments. A rainmaker nurtures cross teamwork to eliminate silos. A rainmaker can energize any team to the highest level of spirited performance.

25. **A communicator.** Great communication was, is, and will be the essential fuel and necessary glue of any organization. Celebrate those who do it well and let them be the model for the organization.

Learn about your specific employees and you will expand this list to 50 or 100 valuable talents. Picture yourself highlighting each team member's talents in a meeting. You then invite them to deliver more of it. "Pat, you're a great communicator. Bring that to the table and help other teammates do what you do naturally." "Murphy, your intuition is so helpful. Help all of us move towards a decision if you see us getting stuck in the data (also known as analysis paralysis)."

Every employee has talents in addition to their occupational skills. When you applaud and invite employees to use more of their talents, you lead and boost morale. Everyone likes to be validated for who they are and what makes them special.

Some leaders resist giving praise and recognition. They claim that a highly positive attitude seems fake. Some of their reaction comes from discomfort with emotion as mentioned in earlier chapters. Yet these leaders are not alone in their view of giving praise. I often hear, "too many smiles and compliments just aren't believable."

Each time I hear it, I ask myself why people find negativity more authentic and easier to trust. Do they think...

■ Negativity can't have a hidden agenda? Although this isn't always true, some people believe that people don't fake negativity. Thus, they find it easier to trust authenticity when they see negativity.

■ Negative emotions are either very authentic or will seem blatantly fake? Many people believe that most anger and sadness come from deep inside. If it isn't deep, they will spot it as fake.

■ They have more to lose by buying into positive fakers? They fear being manipulated by flattery and that makes it tougher to trust positive compliments.

■ Negativity feeds inner doubts? Some people are uncomfortable receiving praise. Although they don't like hearing the negative criticism, it is easier to accept that than hearing effusive praise.

- Life is not perfect? Life is full of imperfections and much pain. People who focus on this belief see highly positive people as nonsensical dreamers. They do not trust them and often don't want to be around them.

- Highly positive doesn't connect? The old saying, misery loves company, may be at play here. These people want others to empathize with their pain not tell them that life is beautiful. However, there are many people who enjoy being around positive people who lift them up.

> **The positive can be just as authentic as the negative.**

To overcome these barriers as you lead morale, make your positive compliments tangible, specific, and real. The above list of 25 talents is tangible. It becomes specific when you apply them to individuals with examples to back it up.

Positive attitudes are authentic when you …

- Show respect for others before you compliment them; it builds trust.

- Make compliments specific and individual.

- Empathize with other's struggles and then light the way with positive opportunities.

- Be vulnerable enough to admit your own struggles.

- Display your optimism with realism. Admit the challenges and then lead everyone to overcome them.

- Be transparent and forthright. One passive aggressive action from you and you will spend a lifetime rebuilding trust.

- Let your actions make your words worthy of trust. Walk your talk.

People don't have to see negativity as more authentic. Through respect, empathy, transparent actions, and realism, a highly positive attitude can be just as authentic as a negative one.

9

Leaders influence.
Cowards manipulate.
Who do you think leads morale?
Which do you want to do?

CHAPTER NINE

Influence, Don't Manipulate

To lead morale, influence, don't manipulate.

Leading isn't about convincing people to think your way. It's about creating a picture of your vision and inviting others to offer their insights. This is leadership influence in action as everyone shares perspectives and also influences how to *achieve* the vision. This leads morale through employee engagement.

The key differences between manipulation and influence are:

Influence, don't manipulate.

Manipulation...

■ Hints/tells (instead of discovers).

■ Spins and skews the truth your way.

■ Disregards other's views and talents.

■ Is opportunistic and driven by selfish gain.

■ Withholds information to further your own angle and purpose.

■ Focuses on people who can serve you; ignores those who can't.

Manipulation undermines and even crushes morale.

Leadership influence...

- Seeks to discover and understand instead of just convincing.

- Draws on your professional people skills to balance communication and care.

- Uses honesty *and* courtesy so people can open their minds and hear you.

- Stimulates other's influence.

- Asks and listens vs. preaches and tells.

- Honors emotions vs. plays on them.

- Respects people for who they are.

- Awakens a vision so everyone can influence the results with their insights.

- Ignites diverse views and opens minds for mega collaboration.

- Goes beyond the moment and echoes far and wide.

Influence lives at the intersection of inspired open minds— and so does morale!

Don't let your misunderstanding about influence stop you from leading morale. Influence is conversation. It's not telling and yelling.

Yet always remember that influence doesn't mean...

- Choosing silence over speaking. It means conversing to explore vs. giving orders.

- Denying your leadership authority. It means unearthing their ideas and views for best results.

- Taking a huge risk with their inexperience. It means mentoring and coaching them with your experience in order to empower them.

- Weakening your leadership. It means developing your strength to trust others.

Influence leads morale. Employees feel respected, engaged, challenged, and trusted. Their morale and commitment soar. Discover and overcome any traps that stop your influence.

Which of these traps are stopping you?

Personality Type

If you are a strong driver, your extreme desire for quick results may lead to you to direct others instead of influencing and engaging them.
Solution: For driver personalities the issue is pace and time. Identify the vision with your teams. Be honest about the deadlines. When you put these elements on the table you are more likely to trust and engage your teams and less likely to drive them.

If you are a strong amiable, your high need for bonded relationships may lead to you to recoil from difficult yet necessary conversations.
Solution: Understand that bonds are not built on avoidance nor broken through honest civil conversations. Your strong ability to empathize will make honest conversations more palatable. This is a talent of yours. Don't run from it.

If you are a strong expressive, your high expressive style may cause others to remain silent. They can't find a moment to speak. It's hard for you to believe this and yet it's true.
Solution: Use a simple people skills rule: the 20 second maximum. If you have been speaking for 20 seconds, pause and wait for input. This simple technique turns monologues into dialogues.

If you are a strong analytic, your high focus on ordered thinking often shuts out those who think creatively or from the big picture. As you tune out or stop them midstream and ask them for the logic and data, they hear you telling them to be you or be silent. This disengages and hurts morale.
Solution: Once again timing is both the issue and the solution. Instead of demanding they use only logic and data, allow them to a) use *their* thinking style and *then* b) discuss the logic and data after that. Two steps instead of one. It engages diverse personalities and still leads to success.

Pressure From Your Boss

When you are focused on influence and engagement and your boss sees it as a weakness, it may cause you to engage your teams less. Don't fall into this trap. It cuts morale off at the knees.

Solution: Ask your leader what specifically they see as a weakness? Have you and your team missed a critical objective? An open discussion about specifics can lead to a better understanding. It prevents you from reverting to your boss' style of directing people instead of engaging them.

Engaging employees is uniquely personal. It is that person-to-person connection that allows you to influence and lead morale. A grand plan at the highest level to engage employees will work when you make it personal—not faceless and generic.

Influence is uniquely personal.

Want an employee's attention? Talk about what they bring to the table. Want an employee's extra effort? Discuss what unique talents each has that you as leader think are valuable. Want an employee to actively engage on a team with a very difficult assignment? Outline how you respect them for climbing the steep hills and enduring slippery slopes.

Generic statements don't engage. Personal discussions do. Consider the following analogy:

Local newspapers for years featured stories about local people instead of filling the entire paper with international and national news. Why? Was it just to keep everyone up to date on local happenings? No. They did it because it engaged more local citizens to buy the paper and to read about their families and neighbors.

Just as all politics is local, all engagement is personal.

Today many businesses do the same by featuring stories about their customers on their social media pages and websites. Others feature pictures and stories about their employees. Personal engages. It leads morale.

What Must Leaders Change to Personally Engage?

■ Replace the old adage "There is no I in team" with "Contribute your unique talents to create team success." It is far more engaging for employees to hear that their personal talents are needed than to be told they are just a cog in a wheel.

■ Honor team members with well-earned individual praise as you point out how each contributed to the team success. Diversity is personal just like engagement.

Over the years leaders neutralized recognition of individual talents to prevent *me-itis*. However, this approach disengages many who are inspired to maximum commitment by recognition of who they are and how that contributes to success.

Coach individual talents into a unity of team success vs. neutralizing individual identities into uniformity.

Guide each employee to learn from each other's strengths. In this they learn how to contribute their personal bests with others.

Change your mindset from that of professional distance to the practice of direct engagement. Great leaders connect and communicate to engage. They don't isolate themselves and justify it with the excuse of professionalism. They overcome any personal discomfort they might have to directly engage for winning results.

> **Generic statements don't engage. Individual discussions do.**

A Winning First Step

1. **Make a list of all the people that report to you.** Next to each name note two of their strengths and one thing that makes them unique. Leave one space blank for something you will discover about them. This exercise starts you practicing individual direct engagement.

2. **Use the information in everyday conversation to engage each person.** It's not about giving constant praise; it's about recognizing their individuality in real time instead

> **Leaders, if you want great morale, engage employees directly; don't isolate yourself.**

of waiting until performance review time. Performance reviews don't engage. Daily connections and discussions do.

Influencing People and Leading Morale Hinges On Why People Work

To lead morale, find out why your employees work. What do they each get out of work beyond the paycheck?

- **Social connection** otherwise they might be working alone. Beyond the paycheck and benefits, these employees want interaction.

- **Security.** Working makes some people feel they are providing for themselves and/or family members. They are unlikely to take a year off and use all their savings to explore the world.

- **Have a voice and a purpose.** Ever wonder why someone, whose spouse makes loads of money, is working for you? They work to have a voice at work and in their own life. They also like having a purpose beyond being a spouse.

- **Appreciation and recognition.** They want to know they matter in this world. Instead of seeing these employees as needy or self-absorbed, see the normal human need to be recognized and appreciated.

- **Making a difference.** Traditionally, many of these employees worked for non-profits. Yet nowadays there are many who choose to work at companies that give back to the world. They would rather work for you than for companies that are not engaged in social altruism.

- **Achievement.** Beyond paycheck and benefits, these employees focus on achieving great things. They crave results.

- **Growth.** These employees hate being stuck in routine job tasks. If they aren't learning and growing, you will lose them.

- **Adventure.** You will find they ask for opportunities to travel or work on global projects. Instead of using these assignments only as rewards, use them to engage these employees now.

- **Creating and innovating.** Traditionally leaders thought this applied only to marketing, advertising, and related creative departments. Yet you will find these creative employees in all departments. They perform best when they can innovate new ideas and create new solutions to existing challenges.

Ask employees why they work instead of assuming it's for a paycheck.

- **What do you get out of work?** What would you like to get out of work? This shows them you are exploring their needs.

- **What inspires you in everyday life?** Is that happening at work? This builds morale engagement currency with them.

- **Beyond the paycheck, why do you work?** Achievement? Growth? Self-fulfillment? Helping others? Living a purpose? Creating and innovating? Listen very carefully to their answers. It is a map to engaging them for maximum success. It is a guide to facilitating teamwork. It tells you what type of recognition and appreciation they want. It even shows you how to help them resolve conflicts and stay productive.

Don't be one of those leaders or managers with no engagement currency. Ask your employees about their motivation for work. Entrepreneur Magazine guest writer Gregg Pollack notes 2013 Gallup research report that millennials and Gen X cite opportunities to learn and grow as a significant factor in their decision to work for you. Go beyond this generational finding. Find out why *your* employees work. Find out what inspires them. You can lead morale far better when you know what inspires your employees to work and commit to the organization.

> Sacrifice is not an order you give. It's an awakening from within.

There is an added benefit for you. These discussions remove the temptation to preach to employees who aren't contributing fully. New leaders sometimes tell employees how much they themselves sacrificed to become a leader. They even highlight what they still sacrifice today to be a leader. They do this in the hope it will get employees to do the same. This doesn't lead morale or inspire contribution because sacrifice is not an order you give. It's an awakening from within.

Reach employees with what they care about AND map it back to team and organization goals. This builds commitment. Specifically,

- Unearth what they think and care about.

- Discuss self-development instead of self-sacrifice.

- Connect their development to how it affects organizational success. It's also a great way to address troublesome behaviors e.g. "When you are late, you let the whole team down."

10

Address bad behaviors. Don't abandon employees by saying, "Work it out yourselves."

CHAPTER TEN

Address Bad Behaviors

As you get to know what each employee cares about, you must also be aware of self-serving employees who care mostly about themselves. Morale depends on motivated individuals focusing on team success. What happens when some motivated individuals focus only on their own success? The dilemma for many leaders is how to handle a high performing self-serving team member.

The Story

One of my customers, a strong leader, described the following leadership dilemma to me:

A team member who produced great results had fallen very ill. I'll call this team member "Reach". When the leader approached the team members for a show of empathy, cards, and flowers for "Reach", many team members quietly avoided the subject and others clearly declined.

Do you tolerate bad behaviors to avoid conflict?

The concerned leader asked me to speak with the team members to learn more about why they responded that way. What had he missed? He wanted to know how to lead them better in the future.

Here's what the team members told me:

1. Reach was well-known for saying things like: "Always associate with people better than yourself to achieve success." Since Reach didn't interact with them very often, the team members wondered who Reach was referring to? They saw Reach overlooking them while always looking upward.

2. Reach helped himself grow but he didn't help others grow. He was well-known for saying, "People give and help because they want to. They shouldn't expect anything in return."

3. Two team members had already spoken (separately) to the leader about Reach's uncaring ways. Both times the leader refocused the discussion on Reach's work results. As the team members compared notes about the leader's response—which they shared with the rest of the team— they all felt it was futile to ever raise the subject again with the leader.

4. When the leader approached them for empathy, cards, and flowers for Reach, they were shocked. They had accepted the leader's results-only definition of teamwork. They had shut out their bad feelings for Reach and simply worked to reach results. The leader's call for a personal show of care for Reach confused them. The leader had betrayed his own reasoning about Reach and had abandoned them as well. The team felt that neither Reach nor the leader showed care toward them.

   They asked me: What is the leader's definition of teamwork? Purely getting the job done or caring for and helping each other to get the job done? The leader seemed to use each definition when it served his purpose and comfort. He focused only on results when they raised issues about how Reach had treated them and then he shifted to the caring definition when Reach was ill.

I reported my findings to the leader without identifying who said what. The leader was stunned to learn that the team members saw Reach as a self-serving opportunist. (This is very telling. The leader had shut out the employees' input.) I asked the leader for his definition of teamwork? He told me he always believed that teamwork included caring and helping each other to grow as well as producing results. I asked him about his results-only response when team members talked to him about Reach's uncaring ways. He confessed he didn't know what else to say when the team members came to him about Reach's bad attitude. He didn't see himself as a *psychologist*. He faced a leadership dilemma and quickly fell back to the traditional results-only focus of teamwork.

Basically, the leader wasn't leading morale. He mislabeled leading morale as being a psychologist and felt uncomfortable and fearful of it. In essence, he hurt the employee's morale as he preserved his comfort.

Tips to Lead Morale in Situations Like This

1. **Be aware of your fears.** Develop your self-awareness. It is a key part of emotional intelligence and it is key to leading morale. Unaddressed fear can stop a leader from growing. This leader's fear of addressing unacceptable behaviors stopped him from addressing Reach's opportunism. Two team members mustered their courage and spoke with the leader about Reach. The leader gave into his own fears, made himself feel comfortable, and hurt morale.

2. **Be aware of team members' behaviors and interactions.** Awareness and listening are critical leadership skills. Reach's beliefs and behaviors were opportunistic yet this leader blocked them out. Even if Reach never behaved this way in front of the leader, team members separately reported it to him.

3. **When situations like this arise, listen to what team members are saying.** Explore further. Ask yourself, "Is this team member (e.g. Reach) behaving as a great team member?" Ask yourself, "What is my definition of great teamwork?"

4. **Speak with various team members and then speak separately with "Reach."** What gaps do you hear when you speak with Reach? Is Reach aware of the behaviors in question and how he is coming across? Level set with Reach about what is expected of him as a team member.

5. **Use any situation like this as a springboard to improve morale.** Create a better definition of teamwork *with* team members so that they can all see it, believe it, and live it. I work with leaders and teams to create a list of specific behaviors that define what it means to be a valuable team member. Doing this creates significant results.

What the leader liked about Reach was his initiative and get-it-done attitude. Yet, an employee can be a high performing teammate who shows initiative for team success *or* a high performing self-serving maverick who initiates for themselves. To lead morale, coach team members on the difference and how to contribute to the team's success.

Self-Serving Maverick Initiators

■ Assume that others agree with what they say.

■ Expect support vs. build support.

■ Suggest a revolutionary new direction in a meeting yet resist discussing it.

■ Jump in without asking others if they welcome help.

■ *Presume* a position of team leadership and claim they are doing it for everyone's benefit.

■ Publicize team efforts without consulting team members on when to publicize.

■ Act from their own view without awareness of other's views or needs. They lack emotional intelligence.

■ Look up and forward—rarely around to their teammates.

Teamwork Initiators

■ Contribute *and* value other's contributions.

> **Teamwork initiators are not self-serving mavericks.**

■ Ask vs. assume. They start conversations and generously listen to all views.

■ Interact to assess which ideas are best: perhaps theirs, perhaps others.

■ See 360 degrees. Their own ideas are but a few in the total picture.

■ Look around before they jump in. If others are active, they offer help vs. take over.

■ Don't presume there must be one leader among them. Equal collaboration is an option.

■ Honor team members and their perspectives. They consult before taking action.

■ Use emotional intelligence as the pathway to true teamwork.

Spot Self-Serving Opportunists! Instead of being teamwork initiators, they...

■ Give half-baked praise of other's contributions.

■ Compliment people personally while ignoring their professional work.

■ Give partial answers to seem collaborative yet withhold more complete knowledge.

■ Sometimes take credit for other's thoughts and ideas.

■ Want others to work hard with minimal investment of their own time.

■ Treat others well to get their help and pull away when others ask for their help.

■ Accept help from teammates and other collaborators but contribute the minimum in return.

Self-serving mavericks and opportunists erode morale. When leaders close their eyes to the impact of self-serving employees, morale suffers. Everyone wants to feel respected and included.

This takes us to the issue of welcoming diversity and including everyone. When employees in the workplace feel excluded, they experience it as a hostile environment and their morale suffers.

To lead morale, unearth any strongly held toxic beliefs about diversity that may be isolating and marginalizing employees. The following toxic beliefs hurt morale:

■ **Differences are either right/wrong.** Differences are neither. Yet because differences can be irritating, people label them as wrong or harmful. It's not a big step from that belief to behaviors that exclude instead of include. Actions like giving plum assignments and promotions to people who are in the majority or to people who are similar to the leaders, exclude diverse employees. This crushes morale.

■ **The opposite of logical is emotional.** Not true. The opposite of logical is illogical defined as errant thinking that produces false results. Illogical is very different from emotional.

Yet leaders and managers who are uncomfortable with emotion wrongly label emotion as illogical. They say "be logical not emotional" and they sideline those who show emotion. They promote people who are like themselves—emotionally unintelligent. As this emotionally unintelligent thinking spreads, it fuels a hostile view of diversity. How ironic! Their focus on logic is the very illogic that brings them to mislabel emotion as bad. Rid your organization of this illogic. Develop your emotional intelligence to lead morale.

- **Those who are different must prove their worth.** This is a dangerous belief on many levels. It promotes the mistaken belief that the business is successful because of the majority—in other words the status quo. However, maintaining the status quo and fearing people who are different undermine success. Businesses thrive when they are ready and able to embrace change. Asking employees who are different to jump through tougher hoops to prove they are as valuable as the majority creates a hostile workplace. It drives away the very talent the business needs in order to succeed. Generational differences, gender differences, personality differences, racial differences, etc... are the rich mix you need in business. Honoring this diversity leads morale and success.

> **The opposite of logical is not emotional. The opposite of logical is illogical.**

When you leave any of these toxic beliefs hidden, you are blind to the hostile workplace that is there. As long as there are no obvious signs like abusive language, racial slurs, sexual innuendo, etc..., you don't see the toxic environment and the related risks to morale and success. Just because you don't see it though, doesn't mean it's not there.

Open your eyes and sharpen your vision. Unearth the toxic beliefs. Don't just look for hostile behaviors and declare all is well when you find none. Toxic beliefs are like bad data fed into a computer. Garbage in, garbage out. Bad data going in creates bad results. Toxic beliefs *in* an organization create a hostile workplace, horrible morale, turnover, and a talent drain.

To lead morale and prevent a hostile workplace:

- **Explore current beliefs.** Don't maintain or recycle the old ones. They may not be worth saving.

- **Unearth assumptions about people.** Discuss the assumptions and replace them with enlightened truths.

- **Spot differences that irritate.** Don't avoid them and tell people to just overlook the irritating differences. Irritation produces pearls. Work through differences to find the gems that make your team great.

- **Check your comfort zone.** The more comfortable you are in your circle as leaders and managers, the greater the chance that team members experience a hostile workplace that you don't see. Step out of your comfort zone. Step into the team members world. See what they are living. Being a leader is not about your comfort. It's about serving those you lead.

- **Develop your emotional intelligence.** Insecurity and lack of empathy foster a hostile workplace.

- **Be aware of the culture club you've created.** Change consultant Alli Polin advises, "Leaders, when you plan a team event for everyone, ask yourselves is it appropriate for everyone? Or does it reflect the leader's preference." She makes a great point. When leaders approach me for team building, I always get input from the team members to help leaders avoid this personal skew.

- **Develop diverse people and their talent.** Don't base standards of excellence on how the majority of employees behave and what they have done. Using the status quo as the standard of excellence does not lead to the future. You will always have new employees whose excellence you must discover, consider, and include. This breeds great morale and great results. Otherwise you and the majority will resist new employees' ideas and live the *we've always done it this way* syndrome.

Tip to Leading Morale:
Reverse a hostile workplace by replacing old beliefs with enlightened truths and developing diverse talent.

As you unearth hidden toxic beliefs, turn your detective skills toward spotting passive aggressive behaviors. Passive aggressive actions are the termites of morale. Passive aggressiveness is an *indirect* expression of hostility.

It is a subtle action to derail others. This subtlety leaves the targets feeling disrespected, disbelieved, and helpless to change it.

Many leaders tell me this is one of the tougher people skills' challenges. They don't want to falsely accuse team members of being passive aggressive. They don't know what passive aggressive evidence looks like so they do nothing. They downplay its effects believing that anything passive can't be that bad. BIG mistake.

Passive aggressive is not less aggressive; it's just less direct.

© 2018 Kate Nasser, CAS, Inc.

Overlooking passive aggressive behaviors helps them flourish with no accountability. It gives free rein to selfish actions. This is a huge trust buster which erodes morale, teamwork, and results.

Spot the pattern of passive aggressive behavior in order to eliminate its ruinous effect on morale and your team's success.

Examples of passive aggressive actions:

- **Interrupting others with a quick "sorry" and hijacking the conversation.** The interrupters don't acknowledge the other people's presence *or* they smile and say to those they are interrupting, "You don't mind do you?" This is not a real question. It is a statement disguised as a question. They are not asking for permission nor showing any true remorse for interrupting. They are hijacking the moment. When someone has a true emergency and needs to interrupt, they first address the people they are interrupting with a heartfelt apology. Then they state the reason for the interruption and are as brief as possible. Fake questions and fake manners are a telltale sign of passive aggressiveness.

- **Restating what another team member already said as if it's their own idea.** Non-passive aggressive behavior would give credit to the team member who originally said it and then add ideas to it.

- **Using subtle sarcasm against another team member and calling it humor.** As the old saying goes, many a true word is said in jest. Team members who use humorous sarcasm to ding others and claim that it's just a joke are being passive aggressive and denying responsibility. They even suggest that their targets are too sensitive and don't have a sense of humor. Yikes! This toxic mess erodes morale and can create a culture of revenge. Humor in the workplace can help morale IF it's shared humor about shared struggles. It hurts morale when it is sarcasm disguised as humor. To rid your organization of this passive aggressive behavior, have discussions about these differences and the impact on everyone.

> **Don't use sarcasm about and against those you lead.**

- **Intellectualizing instead of apologizing.** When faced with evidence of their bad behavior, they are known to say "I wonder why I did that?" instead of "I am terribly sorry." Or they repeat their bad behavior even after they apologize. Intellectualizing vs. apologizing and repeating bad behavior is passive aggressiveness that skirts accountability.

- **Using neutral statements instead of true empathy.** Valuable team members support each other. Passive aggressive team members *appear* to support others. Facing a distraught team member, a passive aggressive would say something like "Yes, it is difficult, isn't it?" A truly supportive team member would say something like, "I feel for you. That is frustrating. How can I help? Let's look at it and find a solution."

- **Holding others to a high standard of teamwork and then *indirectly* threatening them.** A passive aggressive example, "You wouldn't want to be known as someone who didn't help out, would you?" It quietly implies, "I will shame you if you don't help me." If someone were to say this aggressively, it would be: "If you don't help out, I will publicly shame you." Most leaders and team members would see this direct threat as unacceptable. However many overlook the passive aggressive version. Passive aggressive threats are no less threatening. They can even be more damaging to morale as people tell the targets of the aggression that they are too sensitive or must have misunderstood. Hear the passive aggressive threats for what they are—threats!

- **Using apparently logical reasons to undermine other's success and then asking them if they mind.**

  Real life example: A manager asked a team member to present her project updates at the upcoming department meeting. A passive aggressive *team leader* monopolized the meeting and at the end of the meeting said to the team member, "Oh we won't have time for your presentation today. Does it bother you?" Monopolizing a meeting is bad enough. Feigning empathy for the team member she was slighting is passive aggression. The manager said nothing during the meeting to keep it on track nor anything in response to the team leader's passive aggressive behavior. The team member felt disrespected and manipulated.

  Poor meeting management opens the door to passive aggression and poor morale. To lead morale, manage meetings with an inclusive approach that respects everyone's contributions.

Passive aggressive behaviors have the power to demoralize. It's imperative to address these damaging actions in order to lead morale. Here are key steps:

- **Check your own behavior.** Make sure that it isn't passive aggressive. Team members model the leader.

- **Ask yourself, am I afraid of conflict?** If yes, it doesn't mean automatically that you are passive aggressive. However you will probably avoid addressing other's passive aggressive behavior and this hurts morale. Get coaching on overcoming your fear of conflict in order to address passive aggressive behavior, lead morale, and become a far better leader overall.

- **Provide training on how to disagree without being disagreeable.** Some people come across as passive aggressive because they don't know how to disagree directly without insulting others. Yet, a team's diverse opinions are its strength. The way team members communicate honestly and disagree with respect is its lifeblood. Knowing how to communicate well is essential for a culture of high morale and business success.

- **Illustrate the difference between tact/diplomacy and passive aggression.** People using passive aggressive behavior often mislabel their subtle digs as tact when in truth it's venom. Teach everyone how to be honest with care not passive aggressive and venomous.

- **Be willing to spot and address passive aggressive behavior even in a top performer.** A top performer's results contribute a portion of success not all of the success. Team morale is another key component of success and toxic behaviors undermine it.

- **Teach and use engaging meeting management techniques.** Stop bad meeting behavior in its tracks so all will fully engage because they feel valued and respected.

- **Watch for and dismantle cliques.** Not all cliques are passive aggressive. Yet all cliques are harmful to a positive team culture, to morale, and to results.

- **Have the entire team develop a list of** *high performance team member behaviors.* Tangible clear expectations of behavior are one way to develop a culture of positive interaction and give everyone a mechanism for discussing negative behaviors.

- **Above all, don't label people as passive aggressive.** Instead, identify their behaviors as passive aggressive. Highlight the trouble the behaviors create and explore alternate behaviors to effect a change. Labeling people triggers their defensive reactions. Speaking about their *behaviors* calls them to think about what they can change. Many leaders who are especially concerned about labeling people find this focus on behaviors to be a very palatable way of addressing passive aggression.

Passive aggressive is not less aggressive; it's just less direct.

Leaders have an organizational responsibility to engage team members for positive morale and high quality results. You also have an ethical responsibility to create a non-hostile environment where everyone receives basic respect and an opportunity to fully contribute. Passive aggressive behavior is a virus that infects morale and kills results. As a leader, don't be an accomplice by ignoring it and doing nothing.

Strong driver type leaders become an accomplice to passive aggressive behavior with their sole focus on results. They dismiss outcries about the demoralizing behavior with the command: "Just focus on the work."

High amiable type leaders, who love harmony in relationships, often dismiss passive aggressive with, "Oh they didn't mean anything by it." They are now accomplices to this damaging behavior.

Strong analytic leaders may overlook the passive aggressive behavior claiming they don't have enough data to prove it's happening. They become accomplices through the misnomer that if you can't measure it, it doesn't exist. This is a ridiculous claim. Many things exist before we know how to measure them.

High expressive leaders are so connected into the exchange of information they often overlook the impact of *how* things are expressed.

To lead morale, prevent passive aggressive behavior from taking root in the organization or at least spot it and be the cure.

Mislabeling Interaction Trouble as Mere Personality Conflicts

Similarly, there are times when other types of interaction difficulties come to your attention. If you are quick to dismiss it with either, "work it out for yourselves" or "it's just a personality conflict", you put morale at risk.

Your feel-good denials create additional problems. Mislabeling it a mere personality conflict ignites hidden resentments. It fails miserably as it overlooks the true issues to be resolved. Focus on helping people resolve the interaction difficulty before it festers and crushes morale.

Real Life Example

A new leader, whom I will call Bill, joined the leadership team headed up by the hotel general manager whom I will call Lee. Bill had five peers. Each oversaw a different department. These six leaders and their teams had to interact to deliver great customer experience to the hotel guests. During the first week, Bill made many demands on his peer whom I will call Pat. He ultimately said to Pat in private, "I always get *my* way." Pat tried to reset the interaction and suggested to Bill that they work together for the good of the hotel and its guests. Bill took offense and complained to Lee that Pat was uncooperative. Lee brought Bill and Pat together and said, "you two are having a personality conflict."

Bad move. Assuming that two people who are having a conflict are having a *personality conflict* solves nothing. Dismissing interaction trouble as personality conflict intensifies divisiveness. As the real trouble persists, un-addressed issues fester, feed frustration, and lower morale. Resentment grows as the leaders replace the truth with their assumptions of a personality conflict.

It also puts relationships at risk. Pat lost trust in Lee that day and saw Lee as a weak leader who jumped to conclusions. To lead morale in the scenario, Lee should:

- Discover what the trouble is; don't assume what it is. Sometimes this means speaking to each person separately before bringing them together.

- Work with those involved to establish a baseline of honorable teamwork behavior. This includes behavior in shared spaces, teamwork vs. authority based behaviors, acceptable ways to discuss strong views, ways to handle disagreement, and how to handle aggressive and passive aggressive flare ups. When everyone understands what it means to work well together, you can see deviations more easily. You are all then less likely to mislabel trouble as personality conflicts.

- Follow through. Even if you are using Human Resources or outside experts to help address interaction difficulties, stay involved at appropriate points. As a leader, it is your expectation of improvement and your follow-through that bolsters employees' commitment and morale.

Employees tap their leaders for their insight, objectivity, strength, and honesty. When leaders tap dance around the issues or declare the issues unimportant, employees lose respect and trust in the leaders. This hurts morale.

When someone raises an issue about interaction trouble and the leaders quickly pass it off as a personality conflict, people think they are being punished for speaking up. After that, those who raised the issues go into self-protection mode. They close up and grow resentful. This impacts teamwork, performance, morale, and organizational success.

The modern workplace is sustained with core values of respect, honesty, truth, accountability and communication. When leaders twist any situation into something it isn't, it undermines interaction that would otherwise keep the organization moving forward. Whether it's leader to leader, employee to employee, or leader and employee, discover the true issues and address them appropriately to secure the core values of success.

Instead of trying to keep the peace by avoiding necessary conversations and the truth, resolve issues to create a healthy teamwork environment.

Most leaders can see the value in a positive healthy environment. What some leaders don't see is that they must play a key role in creating and sustaining it. This doesn't mean you are babysitting—a metaphor leaders misapply in these moments. You are leading morale.

You are preventing a culture of silence which eats away at morale and a company's success. David Maxfield writes about this in Harvard Business Review, Dec. 2016. He highlights VitalSmarts' research on the impact of not addressing unacceptable behaviors in the workplace. Researchers focused on "failing to confront harsh language, backbiting, bullying, harassment, withholding information, and resistance to feedback and input" and abusive bosses, bad management, and more.

Excerpt:

"Instead of speaking up in these situations, our subjects admitted to engaging in one or more resource-sapping behaviors including: complaining to others (78%), doing extra or unnecessary work (66%), ruminating about the problem (53%), or getting angry (50%).

We found the average person wasted 7 days complaining, doing unnecessary work, ruminating about the problem, or getting angry—instead of speaking up. A shocking 40% of our respondents admitted to wasting two weeks or more.

The hit to the bottom line is even more remarkable. The average person estimated the cost of silence at $7,500, and 20% of our sample estimated the cost of avoiding a difficult conversation to be more than $50,000. Our subjects described ways that silence damages employee engagement, relationships, deadlines, budgets, and culture. Given that the fact that *every one* of our subjects identified at least one costly example, we concluded that it's likely that every employee in your organization is adding to the cumulative organizational cost of silence eating away at your bottom line."

~David Maxfield, *Harvard Business Review,* Dec. 7, 2016

11

Understand what employees need. Treat them the way they want to be treated—not the way you want to be treated.

CHAPTER ELEVEN

Treat Employees the Way They Want to Be Treated

The statistics from VitalSmarts, noted in a previous chapter, show the impact of not leading morale. When leaders overlook employees' needs, employees take to complaining to others, doing unnecessary work, ruminating about the problems, or getting angry. These are unnecessary and costly diversions from productivity and success.

There's no justification and little benefit for leaders to overlook employee needs and avoid addressing trouble. By asking substantive questions, listening to views, observing behaviors, and communicating, leaders can prevent unproductive behaviors and lead morale.

Earlier in the book we explored sixteen emotional needs of employees beyond basic human respect. They represent the often unrequested care employees want from you.

1. The Need to Be Heard	9. Psychological Safety
2. Quiet Listening	10. Devil's Advocate
3. Empathy in Good Times and Bad	11. Knowledge/Data
4. Validation	12. Insight
5. Individual Acknowledgement— They Matter	13. Solutions
6. Outrage	14. Strength and Confidence
7. Support	15. Credit
8. Encouragement	16. Momentum

Of these sixteen, which one do *you* most often want? If your answer is that it depends, then you understand why employees have varying needs as well. If you always want the same thing, remember that not everyone is like you.

The biggest mistake you can make is treating others they way *you* want to be treated. You must treat others the way they want to be treated. If you care enough to learn what they want and follow through with action, you will lead morale. As you learn from one instance to the next, your emotional intelligence and your ability to lead will increase significantly. Your employees, professional colleagues, teammates, friends and loved ones will be impressed and grateful.

> **Create a simple, powerful rule about respect.**

At the organizational level, you can do much to create a safe open place for everyone to engage and contribute. This is essential for high morale.

1. **Create a simple, powerful rule about respect.**
   Respect is key to feeling safe to engage, share, contribute, and innovate. Here is the one simple powerful rule that I developed and have shared with thousands of clients:

   "Respect even when we disagree.
   Civility doesn't weaken the message. It helps others hear it."

   A powerful rule about respect helps everyone to be honest without attacking, demeaning, or insulting others.

2. **Listen!**
   One of the strongest ways to show respect and build respect is to listen. It doesn't mean obey; it doesn't mean agree. It says, I respect you and want to hear your view.

3. **Ask questions to understand vs. judging people to discount their ideas.**
   We open our minds through questions and discussion. Assessing and deciding comes after that.

   Separating these two elements yields tremendous results in leadership and teamwork. Being able to do this is a sign of confidence and maturity.

4. **Celebrate diversity.**

   Applaud diverse ideas. Appreciating different views doesn't mean you agree. It means you are open to learning and exploring. It encourages participation, appreciates people's views, and sustains morale.

5. **Moderate extremes.**

   Extremes are easy. They give that wonderful feeling of achievement. Yet it is often an illusion and extremes can throw everything out of balance. If you see moderation as mediocrity, you may seek excellence only in extremes. You will miss the brilliance of less extreme ideas and the team members who offer them. Your message will be that only extremes have value. You are likely to applaud high extroverts or high analytics or high expressives and overlook the personality types that come across as less extreme.

   Remember, moderation doesn't mean mediocrity. It doesn't mean lack of action. Moderation captures and uses the strength of balance to move ahead without being knocked off course. It takes moderate steps and moderate personality types to produce success. Moderation also helps to sustain morale. Extremes in interaction between leaders and employees can lead to claims of favoritism and discrimination. Can you picture leaders who focus more on some employees than others? This is an extreme that starts a chain of sideline conversations and complaints that undermine the leaders, the teams, and morale.

   > **Moderation doesn't mean mediocrity. It's the strength of balance.**

6. **Encourage self-awareness.**

   Help everyone identify their own pet peeves and own them. Help them to see their own talents and brilliance. Encourage them to share these talents to build a culture of contribution.

Identify slipups in the six steps noted above. Spot the trouble early and call on everyone, yourself included, to correct slipups and renew commitment to morale sustaining behavior.

Fostering a high morale culture where it's safe to engage is worth the effort. It taps the talents you already hired and unearths the human greatness that produces spectacular business results.

Special Case: Morale When Aborting Projects Before Completion

What happens to morale and engagement when a difficult project is suddenly aborted or when a team is reorganized before reaching the project results? What do team members need in this case to sustain their morale and be positive on the next project team?

What employees feel and how can you help them.

When a very difficult project is aborted or a team is reorganized before reaching a successful end, the employees who were truly committed can feel:

1. Angry that you excluded them from the decision.

2. You used them like rats in a maze.

3. They sacrificed for nothing.

4. You cheated them from the finish line.

5. You didn't appreciate their extra effort.

6. You are quietly blaming them for the project failure.

If you want your change leadership efforts to be successful in this moment, you must address these feelings and where they come from.

What Happens to Employees Psychologically During a Very Difficult Project

Employees who rise to a difficult challenge, endure, and perform well, do it by believing that:

- Nothing is impossible.

- Teamwork can conquer any challenge.

- Sacrificing their comfort and personal time will be worth it in the end.

- They will all share in the sweet rewards of success.

In other words, they rule out the possibility of failure to keep themselves going. Think of the US Marines motto: "Surrender is not in our creed." Many employees, especially high performers, subconsciously adopt this belief during difficult projects. When you suddenly abort the project or disband the team, their morale can crash.

Change Leadership: Steps to Address and Sustain Morale Going Forward

1. Most importantly, communicate throughout the project so that employees' expectations adjust along the way. More information and reality throughout the journey reduces sudden shock.

2. Do not blame the team. Sometimes leaders will blame a whole team when a few team members slowed success. Great leaders address underperformers along the way. This leads and sustains morale. Great leaders don't wait and blame the whole team when the project fails.

3. If possible, let project team members be involved in or at least have access to the decision making process.

4. Draw everyone together and discuss what has happened. Mention issues that were beyond their control. Get their thoughts. Highlight the talents and efforts they used. Ask them to recognize each other's efforts during this discussion.

5. In a second team meeting, discuss the lessons learned. If you do the lessons learned in the first meeting, employees may interpret it as "failure analysis". Let them heal with a celebration of talent and effort and then look at lessons learned after that. You can even get their input during the first meeting about how to structure the next meeting about lessons learned.

6. Use disappointing changes and shifts in direction to explore, teach, and develop the team's resilience and agility. Ask for stories from their lives where disappointments made them stronger and wiser. Have them share individual lessons learned. Apply these stories to the next project.

The emotional intelligence you show during these difficult times shows care for employees and inspires future greatness. It's not fluff. It's the tangible steps to re-inspiring and re-engaging employees after a crushing blow. Your efforts strengthen their resilience and re-ignite the drive to succeed.

Lesson: You can pull the plug on a project without pulling the plug on employee morale.

12

Now it's up to you.
Get started!

CHAPTER TWELVE

Now It's Up to You

Now it's up to you. Your beliefs, attitudes, and actions will determine how well you lead morale. As you work through this section of the book, spend some time reflecting on your beliefs, attitudes, actions and how they lead or weaken morale. Beliefs, self-awareness, change, and continuous growth make the difference.

Let's start with your leadership beliefs. Are they helping you lead morale? Answer these questions to raise your self-awareness.

1. **What is your belief about emotion in the workplace?** This affects how you lead and engage diverse employees. It impacts how you assess performance. It influences whom you mentor for leadership positions. Human beings have emotions. If you label all humans with emotions as unprofessional, who will be left working for you? (See previous chapter for more information.)

2. **Are you patient? Do you think patience is valuable?** Or do you think that patience is a synonym for laziness? Remember Edmund Burke's claim: *Our patience will achieve far more than our force.* Learning and moving forward in complex projects takes time. If you crave activity and push everyone, you may demoralize employees who are learning and working to achieve the goals. If you need results sooner, give them extra training and resources to speed the process. Don't push them around and demean them by calling them lazy.

   On the other hand, when employees are resisting change, do you mistakenly back off and mislabel your lack of leadership as patience? This hurts morale as you enable some employees to resist the change that all will ultimately have to embrace. I've seen it happen.

Example: One team member kept asking questions and raising issues with the message that no change was possible until they addressed all the issues. I said to him, "you pose questions to stop the change." He said yes! Once the leader saw the truth about this employee, he started to lead change and lead morale. Learn to spot questions that show interest and those that are meant to resist and stop the change.

Your patience is appropriate when employees are learning and moving forward. It is inappropriate when they are resisting change and you stop leading.

3. **Humility—strength or weakness?** Your belief about humility is very important when leading a diverse workforce. If you see humility as a weakness, it can skew your view of who is performing well, who has leadership potential, and who is valuable. You may exercise a bias for high extroverts and even arrogant mavericks.

List out what you see as high performance and low performance behaviors. Are any of the low performance behaviors on your list actually your view of humility as a weakness? Are the high performance behaviors skewed towards high extroverts or over-confidence? It's especially important to be aware of your skew if you are leading culturally diverse workforce. Some cultures hold humility in high regard. Others mistake it as a lack of confidence. Leaders from all cultures need to see behaviors clearly. If you mislabel employee behaviors, it can hurt them, morale, and performance.

4. **Empowerment—do you believe in it?** How do you define it? Many leaders see empowerment as delegating. Yet delegating isn't true empowerment. It doesn't share power (i.e. em-power). Delegating retains power as it assigns responsibilities.

Others see empowerment as throwing people into the deep end and letting them find their own way. That's not empowerment. It's abandonment.

To empower is to inform with knowledge, mentor for skill development, and share power. It includes collaboration. What is your belief about empowerment? Risk to the business or path to success? Your answer affects whether you will empower and lead morale.

5. **Teamwork—do you truly support it?** How do you respond when maverick top performers don't work with others? Do you accept

it because they are producing results? Or do you hold maverick top performers to the definition of teamwork you espouse. Teamwork initiators will be assessing your leadership beliefs about teamwork through your action or inaction in those moments. Make the wrong choice and you erode morale.

6. **Showing employee appreciation—necessity or nicety?** Employee surveys continue to rank appreciation and recognition as very important. The surveys also show that leaders aren't doing it often enough or giving enough of it. Are you one of those leaders? Why? What are your leadership beliefs about employee recognition and appreciation? To lead morale, you must show appreciation and recognition.

7. **Employee interaction trouble—do you help them work through it?** Or do you label it as immature? Do you snap at them, *work it out for yourselves!* This hurts morale. If they could work it out for themselves, they would. Your response comes across as punishment and that weakens morale. Think about your beliefs and actions regarding employee interaction. Your beliefs drive your actions and the success of the organization.

8. **Collaboration or competition?** Do you think that collaboration and competition can co-exist? Do your actions say this? Or do you think that one is better than the other in business? What type of culture are you creating? Do your employees know that is your goal?

    Many a team is undone by confusing messages from leaders about collaboration and competition. Employees with different preferences will latch on to whichever part of the message they prefer. As a result, teamwork takes a hit. To lead morale and great teamwork, know your beliefs about collaboration and competition. Do you have employees that thrive in the culture you are creating? If not, rethink your approach and communicate.

9. **Inspiration or just the facts?** Is it part of your role as leader to inspire employees? Some leaders see it as essential to leadership and employee engagement. Others see it as a fluffy waste of time.

    Inspiring employees is an important component in leading morale. If you are a "just the facts" type leader, you are leaving the employees alone to inspire themselves. That leaves morale and performance up to chance. If you want an inspired workforce, inspire them. Else why do they need you as a leader? Change your leadership beliefs to inspire excellent performance and high morale.

10. **Intuition—do you value it?** Or do you subscribe to the old saying, "If you can't measure it, it doesn't exist." Think about that statement. Read it over and over. See how foolish it is. There is much that exists in this world before we are aware of it or know how to measure it. If you hold on to the old saying you lower the morale of intuitive employees. They see patterns and solutions to challenges before you do. When you exclude their input because you can't measure it, you hurt their morale and disengage them.

11. **Creativity—do you want it as a culture?** Or do you see creativity as chaotic and unproductive. Today's business focus on innovation requires creativity. Do you truly see the value in it and want it? If yes, do you know how to develop it? A culture of creativity inserts an element of fun and play into work. For many employees this boosts morale. However, if you see creativity and fun as slacking off from work, you will likely squelch it and morale.

12. **People skills—purely common sense or skills to develop?** Do you believe that people skills are inborn in everyone and great interaction is simply common sense? Well, it isn't. Some people show innate talent for great people skills, others do not. Most everyone can learn and develop people skills if leaders invest in it. Does it matter? Yes! It is important to company success. Think about all the differences between people that threaten interaction success. Difficult interactions slow progress and results. I am not referring to productive disagreement but rather to difficult unproductive interactions.

    Great people skills *prevent* difficult unproductive interactions and they help resolve the rest. Develop yours and invest in developing employee people skills. Telling employees to 'just get along' won't fix the trouble and morale will erode. Develop and train their people skills.

13. **Communication—frequent and clear or only when there's a problem?** If you say or suggest to your teams that no news is good news, you will squelch communication. The employees who don't like to communicate

will model you and communicate less. Yet collaboration, teamwork, and results all depend on excellent communication. So does morale.

If you don't like communicating frequently and positively, you may struggle with leading morale. For example, very high driver type personalities often communicate more bad news than good news. They say that focusing on the positive is a waste of time. Another example: Some high introverts find communication draining. They even question the value of it.

To help these introverted leaders, I advise them to compare their needs to the needs of those they lead:
Silence fuels your thinking but communication fuels team members' journey. Your silence can leave others feeling stranded in neutral. When pressure mounts, neutral feels like abandonment to them.

Your silence gives you clarity of thought. Yet it allows confusion to swirl around everyone else. Communication clarifies details, corrects the course, and prevents problems from escalating. Communicate to prevent or at least relieve the stress of confusion and you will sustain morale.

Your silence calms you but unsettles those needing leadership insight. Communication settles and calms them during the struggle. Being in the dark demoralizes and lowers their morale. A tomb is a calm place but hardly inspirational or productive.

Your silence inspires you but it may not inspire those you lead unless they are exactly like you. It disconnects them from you and disengages their commitment. Why should they work through the discomfort of your silence and give their all if they see you living in your comfort zone?

Your silence can come across as uncaring whereas communication shows them you care about them. Take time to tell employees how much you respect them, care about their well-being, and value their talents, commitment, and contributions. Driver type leaders who focus only on results must learn this too. Appreciation and recognition are consistently at the top of employee satisfaction surveys.

The one word of advice I give to introverted leaders about communication is, "sooner."

For extroverted leaders the one word I advise about communication is "pause." People need time to process what you say.

For driver type leaders, the one word I advise is "positive." Instead of leading with *no news is good news,* communicate.

One word of advice for introverts— sooner. For extroverts— pause. For driver types— positive.

Remember, your communication and rapport build employee trust and sustain morale.

14. **Generosity and selfless giving—or faceless anonymity?** Traditional definitions of teamwork stressed, "there is no I in team." It was meant to inspire selfless giving for the good of the team. Years back it worked. Yet what today's younger workforce hears from this statement is: "Who you are doesn't matter." In today's workplace, this is a morale crusher!

Inspire selfless giving by first honoring individual talents and then calling them to maximum contribution. Show appreciation to them and invite them to show appreciation for each other's talents. This helps everyone see that selfless doesn't have to be faceless. Selfless leaders and teammates listen to each other, respect each other, speak with civility even in disagreement, show flexibility, stretch outside their comfort zones, support each other, fill the gaps, and change to produce results. Selfless employees are generous but not faceless.

Now on to your leadership actions. Beliefs drive actions and actions lead morale. Showing recognition and appreciation to employees is one very important action. Many leaders struggle with this idea. They occasionally show appreciation with a generic "good job" comment yet they don't take time to show appreciation and praise employees deliberately. What is the simplest reason to show appreciation to employees? Because you need employees to reach success. I hear leaders say, "Employees are being paid to do a job. It's business, not personal."

This is ridiculous. Employees are not robots. They are people. Appreciation and praise go to the heart of human motivation and contribution.

Showing appreciation lets employees know that the company values them beyond the revenue they produce. It tells the employees that the relationship is not one-way (leader —> employee); it's two-way (leader <—> employee). It shows them they matter. Assuming employees should be grateful for getting a paycheck doesn't lead morale. Showing them that they are essential to the business does.

My Story:

A training company executive called and asked if I would step in and teach one of their courses. One of their instructors had suddenly left and they were in a jam. I jumped in at the last minute, taught the course for them, and the customers were very pleased.

When the training company executive asked me to do more subcontracts for them, I thanked him yet declined. I explained that I had transitioned out of doing subcontracts. I had done that one to help them out of a tight spot. He replied: "Kate, don't bite the hand that feeds you." In that short statement, he made me doubly glad I had declined his offer. He saw the relationship as one-way not two-way.

Don't bully people by saying, "We feed you."

He saw himself as the power broker and saw me as the recipient of his largesse. He, who had the opportunity, was feeding me. It never occurred to him that when I taught the course for them, I was also feeding them. He saw their subcontract to me as alms for a poor subcontractor. He was wrong.

—

Likewise showing appreciation to employees tells them they matter. Their talents matter. Their perseverance in tough times matters. Their initiative to grow, learn, and change matters. If you want to retain employees and their full commitment, show them that you all feed each other. This boosts morale.

In addition to "don't bite the hand that feeds you", eliminate these other phrases that kill morale:

■ *All you've done is...* How demoralizing. The problem is the word "all." Even if employees' efforts fall short of the goal, there's no need to demean them. Discuss what they have done well and what remains to be done.

■ *Don't you think...* This is a statement masquerading as a question. It pretends to be an option yet sneakily demands agreement. It also blocks listening by starting with a negative. It is high pressure with low integrity. If you are going to tell employees what to do, then state it clearly. Transferring your opinion to others as *don't you think*, is presumptuous, patronizing, and rude. *Don't you think…* makes you look like the great pretender. It subordinates others to you and suggests that their views are unimportant.

- **I'm sure you agree…** This is a steam roller technique. It really means, *I am telling you to agree with me*. It comes across as arrogant and deceitful. It kills engagement, contribution, and morale.

- **I'm sorry you feel that way or I'm sorry you feel I have…** When an employee shows the courage to speak up and give you feedback, honor them by listening and responding with sincerity. If you say, *I'm sorry you feel…* you pretend to be considerate while sidestepping accountability. You are saying to employees, you feel that way but it isn't true.

- **I'm sorry you feel that way… and I'm sorry IF I have hurt you…** are morale killers. Listen to feedback. Consider employee perspectives. Discuss the bigger picture if you think that their views are incomplete. Talk about solutions and alternatives. Apologize unconditionally for the impact your words had on them. This builds respect for you and sustains morale.

These morale killing phrases are often a sign of far deeper toxic leadership beliefs and behaviors.

- **Leader negativity.** Negativity drains employees' spirit. They see it as needless difficulty. Employees, especially top talent, want to hear what is possible. They feed off positive beliefs, ideas, and action. Replace negativity with positive discussions and a call to action.

- **Perfectionism.** Perfectionism gets everyone stuck chasing unachievable goals. It reduces the time they have to learn and accomplish achievable ones. Employees see perfectionism as a triple whammy: a) It induces needless stress b) it reduces the quality of their work life and c) it blocks achievement. Replace the scourge of perfectionism with the goal of excellence. Excellence boosts morale through its continued learning and improvement. Perfectionism says, "there's no time to learn—you should already know everything and be perfect."

- **Highly disorganized and unclear.** Why would any employee need a disorganized confusing leader? People can be confused on their own. They don't need a leader who confuses them. A disorganized leader leaves everyone wondering if success is possible, especially when deadlines loom. Clarify vision and call everyone to some form of organized (not necessarily structured) interaction. This clarity leads and sustains morale.

- **Me-itis.** Self-absorbed arrogant leaders drive employees away from them and toward leaders who will appreciate them. Employees tend to love a confident humble leader. Replace the comfort of your me-itis with a focus on employees and what they need and contribute.

Some traditional leaders believe that casting doubt on employees' skills will make employees work harder to prove the leaders wrong. Top talent today sees that as a pointless exercise and a giant waste of their time and talent. They want you to help ignite their greatness through positive means. They want you to inspire, mentor, coach, and give them feedback. They want you to lead morale!

> **Don't demean employees to get them to work harder. Inspire them.**

Positive Means

Communication is a very positive mechanism. To inspire, mentor, coach, and lead morale, leaders must communicate well.

1. **Communicate the big picture.** Don't assume that employees have the same understanding you do from your organizational vantage point.

2. **Communicate the details.** Sometimes leaders get so focused on the finish line, they simply say "do it" and expect everyone to magically create results. Employee morale can dip as they feel abandoned when you omit necessary information.

3. **Communicate completely.** Employee morale suffers when leaders initially communicate only what weighs themselves down. Then at the last minute leaders surprise the employees with additional requirements. Employees feel robbed of a fair chance to reach the finish line successfully.

4. **Communicate that you don't know an answer.** When leaders sidestep questions they don't have answers to, employees get angry. They are raising the issues they see as important. Be straightforward and admit when you don't know an answer. Don't gloss over and sidestep them. Commit to getting the answer and getting back to them.

5. **Communicate outside of your own perspective.** When leaders are experts in their own fields, their expert-itis stops them from communicating clearly to employees who are not expert in those same fields. You can overcome this expert-itis by inviting questions and feedback from employees. They can show you your blind spots—what it is you know that they don't know.

6. **Communicate patiently.** Whether it's from time pressure or personality type, some leaders get annoyed that employees need so much communication. They don't have the patience for it. Just remember, clear and succinct is OK; confusion and silence isn't.

7. **Communicate to fit your employees' needs.** Many leaders communicate the way their leaders communicate to them. This doesn't work with mid-managers and staff employees. The further away managers and staff are from the executive suite, the more information they need to do the work, to stay motivated, and to reach success.

8. **Communicate with an eye toward diversity.** Workplaces are full of different generations, cultures, and occupational experiences. Check your jargon and choose your stories with diversity in mind. Is your communication universally understood? If not, it leaves some employees in the dark and hurts morale. Communicate to include everyone.

Illustration: In an episode of the TV show MASH entitled Life Time, Dr. Hawkeye Pierce is doing a time sensitive operation to repair a lacerated aorta. He wants to graft a part of a deceased soldier's aorta into the patient he is trying to save. The nurse brings him several samples and Hawkeye snaps at her, *no they're too small! You're bringing me spagettini, I need rigatoni. The nurse replies, Doctor, I am part Chinese and part Hawaiian. Can you put that in ethnic measurements I can understand?* Hawkeye replies, *I need an egg roll.*

Communicate to be understood and you boost performance and sustain morale. Nobody likes to feel stupid.

9. **Communicate with preparation.** Some leaders don't prepare enough and don't see the gaps in what they are saying. Others over prepare and become rigid and scripted. Prepare what you have to say and then dialogue with employees to close the gaps.

10. **Communicate without fear.** Some leaders have a fear of public speaking. Even talking to a small group of employees unsettles them. To overcome this fear, focus on how your communication helps employees. It takes you out of your self-focused fear and into care-giving mode.

11. **Communicate both what is going well and the difficult challenges.** When you communicate what is going well, they realize how they have created success. When you communicate what's wrong, the employees can use that confidence to fix the current trouble. That sustains morale.

12. **Communicate to sustain everyone.** Even leaders who communicate information clearly, often don't communicate enough appreciation. Don't take employees for granted or detach from them. Leadership is about inspiring them.

> **To communicate well, remember how much communication sustains others.**

This is especially true when you are leading teams who are virtually dispersed. They may be in different divisions of your company, different states in a country, or in different countries. To lead morale, it is essential that you call them virtual or dispersed teams NOT remote teams. Remote means that they are remote from your central *important* location. This message detaches people, breeds division, and lowers morale. The words *virtual* or *dispersed* mean that everyone matters equally. It inspires commitment and triggers collaboration and contribution.

Do you want your employees to feel like remote controlled drones that you operate from afar? Or a trusted virtual dream team at the heart of company success? Would you want to be on a remote team—i.e. a less important team—or be a part of the important action? Employees want to be seen as equally important regardless of where they are working. This builds and sustains morale. Use the following steps to build a virtual dream team in everyone's hearts and minds.

With virtual dispersed teams:

> **Do not call virtual dispersed teams 'remote teams'. Remote means less important. It kills morale.**

- **Build bonds.** Communicate from the heart and mind. Communicating from the heart shows you care about them as people. It shows respect for their competence and contributions. *If you communicate only from the mind with facts, you can come across to virtual teams as giving orders.* Get to know them as people. Develop an uncommon talent for developing common bonds with face time and fun time. They are both critical to performance and morale.

- **Show commitment and passion.** If you as leader are very laid back with virtual dispersed teams, those teams will see you as uncommitted. If you were in-person with those same teams, they wouldn't automatically see you this way. The distance creates a different perspective. So with virtual dispersed teams, show them your passion for the mission and for their talents. Your passion is the inspiration that renews and energizes them no matter how dispersed they are.

- **Be clear to reduce fear.** Distance can increase team member anxiety and reduce your clarity. As a leader you can sustain morale by being very clear when others are overwhelmed with big demands. Clarify expectations, situations, and issues to relieve their fear. Don't be the boss who demands they relieve your fear while you do nothing to relieve theirs. Leadership and teamwork are a two-way street.

- **Communicate like an explorer.** Respect how employees can enlighten you and explore their views. You are not in every location and there is much they can teach you. Ask great open-ended questions. Listen and explore possibilities with them. Dialogue will correct your tunnel vision and sometimes even prevent it.

- **Mentor and empower them; don't abandon them.** As you lead virtual dispersed teams, mentor with your knowledge, insight, and experience. Empower them to tap their own talents to achieve goals. Likewise, do not dump your responsibilities on them and call it empowerment. It's tough enough to struggle along when resources are nearby; struggling alone when resources are far away can be devastating to the morale of dispersed teams. Mentor and empower them; don't abandon them.

- **Reach out to virtual dispersed teams regularly.** With technology, there is no reason to be detached from them. You can interact regularly with all employees regardless of where they are. It's critical and it sustains morale.

- **Network your inspiration far and wide.** Your words can woo employees to higher levels of achievement or wound them into resentment or apathy. Choose wisely. Be honest not blunt. Celebrate their successes and have everyone learn from mistakes. Build togetherness while respecting individuality. Turn monologues into dialogues.

- **Isolation from distance or differences undermines the true potential of teams especially when dispersed throughout the globe.** Reduce isolation through communication, inspiration, and a unified purpose.

Inspire everyone's commitment by including them in the focus on innovation. So often innovation is the great divide among teams. There are teams that are focused on the excitement of innovation and growth and those that are focused on daily operations. The former feel the importance of their work, the latter often don't. This split can needlessly hurt morale. Even operational teams can innovate to make daily operations better, faster, more cost effective, and more customer friendly.

> **Creativity is diversity of the mind.**

Define innovation and creativity far more broadly than developing and marketing new products.

Help every team see that creativity and innovation are not just wild brainstorms and imaginative slogans done by a few teams. Each employee can contribute their business creativity through:

- Seeing things differently from others

- New ideas

- Incremental process improvements

- Finding common ground in what seems unrelated

- Analytic revelations

- Solving challenging problems with non-traditional solutions

- Storytelling that moves others

- Analogies that teach

- Intuitive insights

They can contribute their creativity:

- In meetings

- In quiet reflection

- At their own desks

- In a drawing

- Through an analytic flowchart

- With serious focus

- Amidst humor and fun

Help them see their unique way of being creative. Awaken what they have to offer. Creativity lifts their morale and lifts them and the organization from the present into the future.

Help them see that their value goes well beyond the department they work in and reaches through the entire organization. As you help employees see that their value goes beyond their job description, their morale soars.

10 Things to Do Right Now to Lead Morale Better Tomorrow

1. **Lead through bonds and relationships not through authority.** People work with those they know, like, and trust. Get to know your teams and let them get to know you. Morale is based in relationships.

2. **Identify and validate your assumptions in every interaction.** Negative assumptions about people can kill morale. Assumptions about people lead to inaccurate deductions and decisions. This creates resentment and mistrust.

> "When you assume the negative, you're angry. If you assume the positive, you will be amazed. Your emotional quotient goes up because you are no longer random in your response."
> ~Indra Nooyri, CEO, PepsiCo

3. **Learn from your mistakes and show them you are improving.** You become a model for continuous improvement and a culture of learning. You become a true morale builder!

4. **Recognize, honor, and celebrate people's talents.** You ignite more contribution and commitment when you highlight people's strengths. It boosts morale.

5. **Put the *we* go before your *ego*.** Generosity and humility are key to leading people and their morale. It builds tremendous trust and respect.

6. **Courageously address necessary conversations.** Unaddressed performance issues, persistent teamwork problems, and crippling organizational challenges, leave team members wondering why you are the leader. Step out of the shadows, out of your comfort zone, and lead morale.

7. **Create calm in a storm without telling others to calm down.** A great leader's presence is like a port in a storm. It shores others up. It doesn't tear others down. It doesn't patronize or demean others for needing support. It buoys them and teaches them how to buoy others and how to sustain morale.

It will be alright

© 2018 Kate Nasser, CAS, Inc.

8. **Develop your inspirational skills.** Many new leaders don't believe they are inspirational. I see this especially with technical leaders. The truth is that inspiring others is a skill you can learn and must develop. Start with understanding what inspires your specific employees. You don't have to be a high extrovert to inspire others. You have to want to inspire others and learn how to do it.

9. **Reach out to learn what your employees think is great leadership.** Ask them to write down the completion of this sentence: "I love it when leaders _____." It's a fun activity to do in a staff meeting. It's easy to answer and teaches you loads of information about your

employees. It also builds tremendous connection. Having them write down their answers before they hear others' thoughts, gives you their true gut feelings. If they all write down a similar answer then you have found an interesting trend and a good starting point.

10. **Develop loads of self-awareness.** Self-aware leaders regulate their extremes and prevent blaming and dumping on their employees. This builds and sustains morale.

Why is continued self-awareness and self-growth so important? Because people leadership is a call to serve others not a reward for your years of service. It requires you to know yourself, give of yourself, stretch yourself, and improve yourself.

It tells them that you too face the challenges of keeping your morale high in good times and bad. It shows your employees that you are not just telling *them* to show team spirit. You are doing it within yourself and helping them to do it.

> **Leading change within yourself changes everything.**

Leading change from within yourself shows them your authentic passion to change what weighs you and them down. It also shows them how you can all change your attitudes when you can't change the situation. Your action-oriented willingness to change shows employees that morale is all about assessing, thinking, and acting. It's not about sitting still and feeling like victims.

You will also help others see the impact of their actions by being accountable for yours. This is so important for maintaining morale. Morale can dip when there are interaction struggles between employees. There are some employees who are only aware of their impact on others when they *see* the impact of their actions. Yet, their delayed awareness leaves scars that hurt morale.

Over the years, I have worked with many of these folks. They are either: not intuitive, focus only on the present moment, or have detached from others for various reasons. You can slowly change this harmful behavior. Coach these folks to consider their impact before they act. Share the leadership challenges you have in interacting with so many people. Let your stories show them how you have learned to consider your impact in advance.

To lead morale, be accountable. Walk the talk.
Make your words come to life with your actions.

For example: A customer support center leader had one agent who was shirking responsibilities for taking calls. The agent chose to only handle emails. This had a tremendous impact on the call queue, on other the workload of other agents, on their morale, and on customer satisfaction about hold times. *After many discussions with this agent and no change in behavior,* the leader removed the agent's access to the email queue. The leader was uncomfortable doing it because it wasn't her natural style. Yet she did it anyway. She took steps that made her previous words come to life. She was accountable as a leader.

The leader explained to the agent that she had to do it to improve the support center's performance. The agent's actions were hurting customer satisfaction and team morale. As the workload balanced out, the morale of the other agents rose. The agent in question, although not initially pleased with the leader's action, admitted that she needed that type of restriction in order to change her behavior and focus on calls. One small change in the leader's behavior influenced an agent's behavior change. It also benefited the team's morale, the whole contact center, and the customers.

When you handle tough issues, employees can respect you and your efforts in leading morale. You become the model of continuous improvement, accountability, and a positive can-do attitude.

As a role model, you can help everyone overcome another big morale challenge—the baggage of the past. Old hurts, insecurities, feelings, scars, and unaddressed situations are psychological baggage that drag morale down and slow success. Help them to see:

> These mountains that you are carrying,
> you were only supposed to climb.
> *~ Najwa Zebian*

Yet telling them to just get over it doesn't lead morale. To offload the baggage and lead morale, help employees identify what is weighing them down. Are they carrying...

1. **Extreme need for validation.** This can paralyze people. Being accepted is a normal human need. It represents connection and belonging. Yet people must balance this with self-worth and self-confidence. Reinforce their talents and have them do a daily confidence sheet to build theirs.

2. **Undefined values.** Wandering may be good for relaxation, yet endless wandering becomes a weight in life. Dissatisfaction becomes a generalized feeling of discontent and then anger. I have helped many dissatisfied employees identify what it is they value. It has changed their attitude at work. In some cases they made modest changes that uplifted them. In others, they changed jobs and found satisfaction in work that most closely matched their values.

3. **Resentment and grudges.** It's normal to feel them yet toxic to carry them. They divert energy to past events. Once the trouble has been addressed, move on.

> Forgiveness means giving up all hope for a better past.
> *~Lily Tomlin*

4. **Revenge.** This relative of resentment controls even more energy. When leaders or teammates seek revenge, morale plummets to its lowest point. Keep morale high by fixing the trouble, moving on, and not entertaining thoughts of revenge. You can't get to the future by seeking revenge on the past.

5. **Psychological scars.** The scars from employees feeling disrespected and demeaned can crush morale. Identify the scars and work through them. Change your behaviors to prevent new scars. Seeing changes in behavior helps everyone trust and move on with a positive attitude.

> Whatever is rejected from the self, appears in the world as an event.
> *~C.G. Jung*

6. **Past challenges that others didn't have.** When some employees see that others have had an easier time at succeeding, they feel weighed down and isolated. To change, ensure a level playing field going forward or morale will suffer. Eliminate age bias, gender bias, racial bias, pay inequity, and favoritism. You can't change the tough challenges of the past; you can definitely help everyone succeed going forward.

7. **Unfairness.** Resolve unfairness by having employees speak up when they see it. Listen to them instead of trying to prove them wrong. Take up the challenge of creating a more fair environment.

8. **Jealousy.** Unaddressed jealousy can eat away at morale like a hidden virus. Jealousy hurts the employees who are jealous, the employees they are jealous of, and the team's morale. I've seen too many leaders write off jealousy as a minor annoyance. This is a big mistake in leading morale. Employees and teammates must collaborate and work together. How can they do this if one or more are jealous of the others?

   Jealousy is the feeling that you've lost something. If an employee loses out on a promotion to another teammate, don't disrespect them by saying "oh you're just jealous." Instead, give them the specifics of why the other employee was chosen *this time*. Boost their morale by helping them see their value, their talents, and opportunities for them to succeed. Jealousy is often based on a zero-sum belief that if one person wins, one has to lose. Show them this isn't true. There are multiple opportunities for success. Help them determine if a zero-sum belief is creating their disappointment. Then allow them time to digest it and meet with them again. If the jealousy is a more generalized fear of losing out, the real issue may be envy.

9. **Envy.** Envy is the feeling that you lack in some way. It shows a lack of self-love and self-confidence. To minimize the challenge of envy, honor individual talents. Encourage everyone to value their own talents. Call on each employee to use their talents to climb the mountain of success. Everyone counts. Everyone matters—not just the star performers.

Jealousy and envy are true morale killers.
Address them to lead morale.

Remember, engage employees in concrete discussions to stop interaction troubles from hurting morale. It is never too late to leave the baggage behind and travel forward together with great morale.

© 2018 Kate Nasser, CAS, Inc.

Conclusion—From Beginning to End

At the beginning of this book I asked you to think of one word—dignity. I asserted that morale is all about dignity. When I started writing the manuscript, I didn't start with that thought. I wrote the manuscript and then came across a book entitled *Dignity at Work* by Dr. Randy Hodson (Cambridge University Press, 2001). As I read it, I realized that what I had written was all about dignity. So I went back and inserted that page at the beginning of this book, Leading Morale. Now at the end of this book, I offer you the connections between dignity and morale.

To do this, I quote the late Dr. Randy Hodson, Professor of Sociology at The Ohio State University. He dedicated his book, *Dignity at Work*, as follows: "To workers everywhere whose dignity can be challenged but cannot be denied." This statement at the start of his book sums up the very reason why you must lead morale. Employees will always stop you from denying their dignity.

When you are not leading morale, your actions and other happenings in the workplace challenge and even assault employees' dignity. And how do employees respond? According to Hodson, they resist the denial of dignity. When you are not leading morale, your direct and indirect workplace assaults on their dignity put employees into resistance mode. Does your leadership vision include "get employees to resist?" I doubt it. And if you are leading *change*, resistance is a death knell.

Now imagine instead that you are leading morale using the steps, attitudes, and behaviors outlined in this book. You are engaging everyone to set and reach goals. Hodson stresses the importance of this "bilateral engagement" in maintaining dignity at work. Most importantly, he says that the goals must include maintaining employee dignity.

As you engage employees and the workplace feels less hierarchical, employees feel more meaning and belonging at work—a key part of dignity.

This is especially important to millennial workers. Yet with less hierarchy and more peer-to-peer collaboration, co-worker issues arise that also assault dignity. You must help co-workers resolve these issues. Then help employees/teams develop the know-how and norms to address these dignity assaults among themselves in the future. Both steps are essential to leading morale. If you refuse to help them, they resist the assaults through avoidance and other measures. Trust and productivity drop because you refuse to lead morale.

> "Compared with people at low-trust companies, people at high-trust companies report: 74% less stress, 106% more energy at work, 50% higher productivity, 13% fewer sick days, 76% more engagement, 29% more satisfaction with their lives, and 40% less burnout." ~Paul J. Zak, The Neuroscience of Trust, Harvard Business Review, Jan. 2017.

To lead morale well from beginning to end, show respect in every move you make. Human respect honors employee dignity and builds trust. Speak honestly with courtesy and civility. Serve those you lead with confidence and humility. Acknowledge their talents, engage them all, help them resolve teamwork issues, and thank them for their contributions. This leads and sustains morale.

Replace the old belief that trust is mostly about your knowledge and educational degrees. The reality is that your trustworthiness as a leader is about your integrity and how you treat others. Using your emotional intelligence and showing deep human respect for employees is key. Without that, your IQ, occupational knowledge, and educational degrees mean little to employees.

Engage employees, honor their dignity, and build their trust to lead morale. And always remember...

If you're not leading morale, you're not leading anyone.

References

Maor, D., Reich, A., Locarini, L., The People Power of Transformation, McKinsey & Company, Feb. 2017, https://www.mckinsey.com/business-functions/organization/our-insights/the-people-power-of-transformations

Zak, P., The Neuroscience of Trust, Harvard Business Review, Jan. - Feb. 2017, https://hbr.org/2017/01/the-neuroscience-of-trust

Shelley, L., Why Belonging is Key in Today's Workplace, Digitalist Magazine, Dec. 2014, http://www.digitalistmag.com/lob/human-resources/2014/12/03/why-belonging-is-key-in-todays-workplace-01829011

Cranston, S. Keller, S., Increasing the Meaning Quotient of Work, McKinsey Quarterly, Jan. 2013, https://www.mckinsey.com/business-functions/organization/our-insights/increasing-the-meaning-quotient-of-work

Knicks, D., Empathy is the Hottest Trend in Leadership, Time.com Money Section, June 21, 2016, http://time.com/money/4376423/empathy-leadership-trend/

Goleman, D., Positive or Negative? It's Your Choice, Sept. 2016, https://www.linkedin.com/pulse/positive-negative-its-your-choice-daniel-goleman

Maxfield, D., How a Culture of Silence Eats Away at Your Company, Harvard Business Review, Dec. 2016, https://hbr.org/2016/12/how-a-culture-of-silence-eats-away-at-your-company

Pollack, G., Why a Culture of Personal Betterment is Competitive Advantage, Entrepreneur Magazine, Sept. 2015, https://www.entrepreneur.com/article/250180

Hodson, D. (2001). *Dignity at Work*. New York, NY: Cambridge University Press.

Acknowledgments

Special thanks to the professionals who helped in the production of this book:

Kimb Williams of Kimb Williams Graphic Design, for the compelling book cover design. For many years, Kimb has enhanced the visual presence and impact of my business with her creative talents. I turn to her repeatedly for every graphic design need.

Illustrators Joy and Tom Guthrie of Vizwerx Group, LLC, whose artistic creativity brought the messages and concepts in this book to life. I am also tremendously grateful for their stellar communication skills and customer focus which made the process of working together highly productive, easy, and enjoyable.

Carla Green of Clarity Designworks, whose design layouts make reading this book an engaging experience for all.

About the Author

Long time clients of CAS, Inc. say that Kate Nasser's workshops are a spiritual experience. "As you and your colleagues engage with her in workshops, the deeper greatness in you emerges and there's no going back."

For more than 25 years as President of CAS, Inc, Kate has delivered workshops, keynotes, and consultations on leadership, teamwork, employee engagement, and service, to companies in diverse industries around the world. She is known for her authenticity, humor, energy, wisdom, inspiration, and yes, tangible results. Kate's natural intuition (her GPS about people as she calls it) uncovers people's hidden issues and moves them with a special oomph to new views and actionable changes. Kate's inspiration and years of experience provide the guidance that people welcome when moving from the status quo to desired advances and clear-cut results.

Whether she is addressing the challenges of leading morale, engaging employees of different generations and cultures, strengthening teamwork, or improving customer service, Kate's uncanny ability to adapt and work with anyone is the constant that delivers definitive results.

Why do clients trust her and keep coming back for more guidance? Because she is a top-notch communicator, an experienced results-driven consultant, and a highly balanced professional who combines brainpower and heart in all that she does. In short, she understands them and delivers what they need. She is the best at teaching professional people skills for leadership, teamwork, and service.

On top of that, Kate has a Masters in Organizational Psychology, Bachelors in Mathematics, previous corporate employment at Johnson & Johnson before founding CAS, Inc., and an insatiable curiosity that keeps her learning. Conference committees tap her high-energy interactive talks to give their participants extraordinary sessions. When you work with Kate, every session has novel insights to move you forward.

For more information on Kate's services and programs, go to *KateNasser.com*. Join her on Twitter (@KateNasser) in her weekly #PeopleSkills global chat still trending in its 6th year and read her posts on LinkedIn (KateNasser). To see her in action, go to her YouTube channel (Kate Nasser) and then book her for your event.

Kate welcomes your questions and insights via email through her website. She looks forward to interacting and working with you especially in her new workshops on Leading Morale.